MINNESOTA
GEOGRAPHIC
SERIES

MINNESOTA
PORTRAIT OF THE LAND AND ITS PEOPLE

By Patricia Condon Johnston

© 1987 by American Geographic Publishing
Helena, Montana

William A. Cordingley, Chairman
Rick Graetz, Publisher
Mark Thompson, Director of Publications
Barbara Fifer, Assistant Book Editor

ISBN 0-938314-36-X
© 1987 American Geographic Publishing
Box 5630, Helena, MT 59604 (406) 443-2842

Text © 1987 Patricia Condon Johnston
Design by Linda Collins.
Printed in Hong Kong by DNP America, Inc., San Francisco

Library of Congress Cataloging in Publication Data

Johnston, Patricia Condon.
  Minnesota : portrait of the land and its people / Patricia Condon Johnson.
    p.   cm. — (Minnesota geographic series ; no. 1)
  Summary: A geography of Minnesota, with chapters on geology, history, and the six regions that comprise the state, and sketches on notable sights.
  ISBN 0-938314-36-X (pbk.) : $14.95
  1. Minnesota—Description and travel—Juvenile literature. [1. Minnesota—Geography.] I. Title. II. Series
F606.3.J64 1987
977.6—dc19   87-25086
                                                         CIP
                                                          AC

PREFACE

I am really delighted that American Geographic's publications director Mark Thompson asked me to write this book about Minnesota. I have lived in Minnesota my entire life, as did my parents before me. My antecedents include immigrants from Germany, Norway and Ireland who came to Minnesota. Both my husband Charlie and I grew up on the fringes of Scott Fitzgerald's Summit Hill neighborhood in St. Paul. And we chose to bring up our four children in Minnesota.

To my mind, there is no finer place to live than Minnesota. The center of my personal universe, it is moreover a national center for industry, education, medicine and the arts. Just for the record, there are four times as many millionaires per capita in Minnesota as in Texas. There are more theatergoers per capita in the Twin Cities than in New York City. And the Minneapolis/St. Paul campus of the University of Minnesota has the largest enrollment of any single campus in the United States.

Speaking to its considerable natural beauty, Minnesota is a land of remarkable contrasts. Refreshing lake-studded pine forests to the northeast give way to fertile prairie farmscapes in the southwest. Living up to a reputation as the land of lakes, Minnesota has more lakes than any other state, also more miles of recreational shoreline than California and Oregon combined. But the statistic that I like best says that Minnesotans live longer than people in any other state save Hawaii. (My own grandmother is 96, and looks forward to her 100th birthday.)

A great many people throughout Minnesota helped with this book, answering my endless questions and providing useful data. Thank you, all of you, enormously. My husband Charlie did some of the beautiful photography for this book, and he also deserves special mention for providing the nurturing environment in which I work. I appreciate you more all the time, Charlie. I am grateful to John Borchert, Regents' Professor of Geography at the University of Minnesota, who saw this project through with me from beginning to end. His pointed questions helped guide and shape the manuscript, making this a far better book than it would have been without his help. And I sincerely appreciate editor Barbara Fifer's close attention to both facts and grammar.

I'd like to dedicate this book to my mother, Betty Condon. It was she who first taught me to love geography.

CONTENTS

Title page: Boundary Waters Canoe Area. B.A. FASHINGBAUER
Facing page, clockwise from upper left: Fall farm scene. R. HAMILTON SMITH; *Boundary Waters canoers.* DANIEL J. COX; *St. Louis River, Jay Cooke State Park.* R. HAMILTON SMITH; *railyard and Capitol, St. Paul.* R. HAMILTON SMITH

Left: Pipestone Creek at Pipestone National Monument. JEFF GNASS

Cover photos: left top: Nicollet Mall in Minneapolis. DANIEL J. COX. *Left bottom:* The Duluth aerial bridge lifts for an incoming ore boat. R. HAMILTON SMITH. *Center:* Voyageurs National Park. STEVE KAUFMAN. *Right top:* White-tail buck. DANIEL J. COX. *Right bottom:* Speed skating at the St. Paul Winter Carnival. R. HAMILTON SMITH *Back cover:* Birches. TOM TILL

SHAPED BY STREAMS

Above: *Red maple leaves.*
D. CAVAGNARO

Right: *Fog on St. Croix River, now a federally-designated Wild and Scenic River, once a highway for furs and, later, timber.* TOM TILL

Minnesota inhabits the very heart of the North American continent, and its myriad streams and rivers, attesting this centrality, flow in three directions. Near Hibbing in northeastern Minnesota, three gigantic watersheds meet corner to corner in the Giants Range. An ancient granite ridge that rises 400' above the surrounding glacial plain, the Giants Range runs in an east-west direction for 50 miles. Except for Triple Divide Peak in Glacier National Park, this is the only three-way continental divide in the contiguous United States.

Streams on the north slope of the Giants Range flow north through the Red and Rainy rivers to icy Hudson Bay in Canada. Streams on the south slope flow eastward into Lake Superior, ultimately reaching the Atlantic Ocean via the Great Lakes and the St. Lawrence River. At a point identified by a marker on a western spur of the Giants Range, both these drainage basins meet the immense Mississippi watershed, the largest in Minnesota and in the country. Draining all or parts of 31 states, including more than half of Minnesota, the Mississippi empties into the warm-watered Gulf of Mexico.

Minnesota's waters and water highways have been its fortune, defining the borders and shaping the state's destiny. The greater portion of Minnesota's northern boundary is an early voyageurs' canoe route that connects Lake Superior to Lake of the Woods using the Pigeon and Rainy rivers and numerous lakes Minnesota shares with Canada. To the east, Lake Superior, and the St. Louis, St. Croix and Mississippi rivers, delimit Minnesota. Its western boundary follows the strategic path of the Red River and Big Stone and Traverse lakes.

Minnesota's rivers were the thoroughfares of Indians who located their villages along lakes and streams. As early as the 1600s, they became avenues of commerce for French fur men using birchbark canoes copied from the Indians. Later, facilitating white settlement, these water highways brought immigrant families to Minnesota homesteads. That Minnesota became a great state can be traced to the waterpower that operated its first sawmills and flour mills. In the 1980s, Minnesota's rivers continue as major navigation routes. They provide drinking water for homes and water for industrial purposes including electric power production, and their recreational value is significant. Tourism is a ranking industry in Minnesota.

Queen of Minnesota rivers, the Mississippi is also America's greatest river, carrying fuel, food and building materials through America's midlands. Taking its name from an Algonquin word meaning "great water" when applied to rivers, it begins as a clear, shallow stream in the wild rice beds of Lake Itasca in north-central Minnesota. Meandering through pine-forested wilderness and prairie farmland to the Falls of St. Anthony at Minneapolis, the northern reach of the river was an important fur trade canoe route. Later, it was a main artery for log transportation until the big timber was exhausted.

In 1680, while he was being held captive by the Dakota Indians, Father Louis Hennepin "discovered" St. Anthony Falls, the most abrupt drop in the Mississippi's entire 2,350-mile course. Having accompanied La Salle's expedition to America in 1675, Hennepin and two com-

panions had fallen into the hands of the Indians at Mille Lacs Lake. While one of the men was held hostage, Hennepin and the third man were allowed to travel down the Mississippi as far as the Wisconsin River where La Salle had agreed to drop supplies. It was during this voyage that they first saw the waterfall that Hennepin named for his patron saint, Anthony of Padua.

One hundred fifty years later, the waterfall gave rise to sawmilling and flour milling, begetting, in the bargain, the twin cities of Minneapolis and St. Paul. When man-made aqueducts, dams and canals threatened to destroy St. Anthony Falls earlier in this century, it was stabilized by a concrete apron that unfortunately nearly obliterates its natural beauty. Current Minneapolis developers are renovating and rebuilding the Minneapolis waterfront in

HENNEPIN AT THE FALLS OF ST. ANTHONY, AD 1680. *Oil painting by J.N. Marchand. Owned by Dr. James E. Trow, Minneapolis.*
MINNESOTA HISTORICAL SOCIETY

Pembina
Lake of the Woods
Thief Lake
Mud Lake
Agassiz National Wildlife Refuge
East Grand Forks
Upper Red Lake
Lower Red Lake
Crookston
NORTHWEST
Cass Lake
Bemidji
Itasca State Park
Itasca Lake
Leech Lake
Park Rapids
Moorhead
Detroit Lakes
Grand Mound
International
VERMILION IRON RANGE
Boundary Waters Canoe Area
Voyageurs National Park
Ely
GUNFLINT IRON RANGE
Grand Portage
IRON RANGE
Tower
Grand Marais
Mountain Iron
Virginia
Lutsen
Chisholm
Hibbing
ARROWHEAD
Grand Rapids
CUYUNA IRON RANGE
Two Harbors
Lake Superior
HEARTLAND
Duluth
Brainerd
Mille Lacs
Little Falls
Alexandria
Pine City
Browns's Valley
Big Stone Lake
Graceville
Sauk Centre
Glenwood
St. Cloud
Lac qui Parle
Willmar
Litchfield
Mississippi R.
Stillwater
Lake St. Croix
Buffalo
St. Paul
Minneapolis
Fort Snelling
Hastings
New Prague
Redwood Falls
Red Wing
Lake Pepin
Northfield
Nerstrand State Park
Wabasha
SOUTHWEST
Pipestone National Monument
Cannon R.
Mankato
Pipestone
Jeffers
Rochester
Winona
SOUTHEAST
Lanesboro
Forestville State Park
O.L. Kipp State Park
Blue Mounds State Park

the once heavily industrialized St. Anthony Falls district to include residential and office space, festival markets, restaurants and parks that reflect the area's historic past.

Downstream from St. Anthony Falls, the Mississippi takes on dramatic new dimensions. Gathering water from numerous tributaries, it becomes many times wider, flowing south to Iowa through a deep, broad channel encased by steep-walled limestone bluffs. French fur posts once stood on its shores; later, picturesque river towns were birthed in the steamboat era. South of Lake City, the Upper Mississippi River Wildlife and Fish Refuge embraces nearly 194,000 acres of diverse floodplains on both sides of the river stretching almost to Rock Island, Illinois. A stunning example of what a wildlife refuge can be, this water and wetlands area shelters some 270 species of birds, 50 mammals, 45 amphibians and reptiles, and 113 kinds of fish.

Tributary to the Mississippi, the Minnesota is the largest river wholly within the state. Originating in Big Stone Lake on the South Dakota border, it flows eastward in a large "V" through rich, fertile bottomlands in southern Minnesota to where it joins the Mississippi at Fort Snelling. Both French and British fur traders thought it might lead them to the Northwest Passage. The French knew it as the St. Pierre's River, but the British and early Americans later dubbed it the St. Peter's. Today its Indian name prevails. Minnesota is a Dakota word, commonly translated as "land of sky-blue waters." But this isn't exactly what the Indians meant. To the Dakotas, Minnesota meant cloudy waters, which is how the river looks at flood stage with light-colored clay suspended in its water. Translated into English, Minnesota became "sky-tinted waters."

To the east, forming a portion of the Minnesota-Wisconsin border, the clear St. Croix River is one of the most picturesque streams on the continent. Named for a French trader, one Sainte-Croixe, it cascades through wilderness valleys and sharply-cut glacial gorges. Formerly a fur trade route helping link the Mississippi and the Great Lakes, the St. Croix later was appropriated by lumbermen who cut the vast stands of white pine on the river's upper reaches, floating the logs downriver to sawmills at Stillwater, Winona and St. Louis. Presently, the St. Croix is federally protected as a wild and scenic river, one of eight such rivers in the nation. Because it is within a day's drive for millions of people, it is an exceptional

recreational resource, attracting boaters, campers, climbers and canoeists.

On the opposite side of the state, the Red River of the North (to differentiate it from the Red River flowing between Texas and Oklahoma) is an altogether different kind of river. Draining an extinct glacial lake bed, it flows north from Lake Traverse to the Canadian border, separating Minnesota from North Dakota. The Red River isn't

the least bit red, and no one has ever waxed poetic about this river's natural beauty. As it wanders tortuously across pancake-flat, treeless plains, the Red River is usually muddy, even badly polluted in some stretches. Encased in steep, barren clay banks, it is certainly not attractive.

The plain fact is that beauty is not everything, however. The Red River drains some of the richest black farmland on earth. By the 1890s the area's huge bonanza

The Minnesota River, seen here at Lac Qui Parle, is the longest tributary of the Mississippi within the state.
R. HAMILTON SMITH

7

wheat farms had made it the bread basket of the world. Still a cash crop region, and still growing wheat, the Red River Valley also produces potatoes, sugar beets, sunflowers and vegetables.

Minnesota is the 12th largest state in the Union, covering 84,068 square miles, 4,059 of which are water. With more lakes than any other state, it is second only to Alaska in total water area. Hands down, its most spectacular lake is Lake Superior.

Shared with Wisconsin, Michigan and Canada, Lake Superior is the largest freshwater lake in the world. The Ojibwe called it "Kitchi Gamma" or great water, and Henry Wadsworth Longfellow hailed it as "shining Big-Sea Water" in his *Song of Hiawatha*. Boldly beautiful, yet fickle enough to break large seagoing vessels, Lake Superior is a north-country siren, annually drawing untold thousands of vacationers to its rocky, wave-lashed shores. Since 1959, when the St. Lawrence Seaway (the world's longest artificial seaway) was widened to accommodate ocean-going vessels, Duluth, its western terminus, has become an international port. It harbors freighters from numerous countries, including Great Britain, Norway, the Netherlands and Japan.

If you believe the state's license plates, Minnesota has 10,000 lakes. Actually, the figure is more than that. Currently, Minnesota has 12,034 lakes, and this is down from a few years ago when there were 15,291, many lakes since having been drained as man keeps tinkering with the landscape. As defined by Minnesota's Department of Natural Resources, a lake is any basin at least 10 acres in size that is partially or completely filled with water. All of Minnesota's 87 counties, save Rock County in the southwestern corner of the state, have natural lakes. The largest lake wholly within the state is Red Lake. A remnant of Glacial Lake Agassiz in northwestern Minnesota, it covers 288,800 acres, with 123 miles of shoreline. Minnesota has a whopping 90,000 miles of lake and river shoreline.

So it is little wonder then that nearly half of Minnesota's 4.2 million residents are anglers. Or that on weekends from May through October, Minnesotans en masse head for the lakes, trailing their boats behind them. More people probably fish for crappies and sunfish (silver bass) than for any other species, and even with generous limits—15 crappies and 30 sunfish—the supply remains constant. Just for the record, Minnesota hatcheries raise

and stock 250 million fish annually—walleye, northern pike, muskellunge (muskie), bass, panfish, catfish and trout.

The state fish is the walleye, which can weigh up to 17 pounds, and is most at home in the larger, clear cool northern lakes. The best muskie waters are the Mississippi headwater lakes in north-central Minnesota and the river itself, especially between St. Cloud and Brainerd. Northern pike, close cousins to the muskie, lurk in nearly all types of Minnesota water, including cold- and warm-water lakes and slow-flowing rivers. Trout enthusiasts head mainly for streams that run into Lake Superior. Southeastern Minnesota's rugged hill country also has some excellent brown-trout streams.

Icy terraces on the shore of Lake Superior, seen here at sunset on Stoney Point, were created by the lake's wave action. DANIEL J. COX

Facing page, left: *Young fisherman with catch of walleyes in Boundary Waters Canoe Area.* B.A. FASHINGBAUER
Right: *Walleye statue at Garrison in Heartland lakes region.*
R. HAMILTON SMITH

Above: *Proud farmer with corn harvest. Minnesota's corn is primarily a feed crop for pork and beef production.*
Right: *Wheat, the basis of pioneer agriculture here, remains a staple Minnesota crop.*
R. HAMILTON SMITH PHOTOS

Minnesota's primary natural resources—tall timber, fertile soil and iron ore—all were critical to the state's development. When Minnesota was admitted to the Union in 1858, its leading industry was lumbering. White pine grew in every Minnesota county east of the Mississippi, often reaching a height of 160' with a diameter of 30" or more. Significant by itself, the lumber industry also was the first in the state to generate large amounts of capital; it helped develop such industries as flour milling, railroading and banking. Because of St. Anthony Falls, Minneapolis was the state's lumbering capital with 13 mills. Once the railroads reached the prairies in the 1870s, Minnesota white pine built entire cities on the western frontier, including Bismarck, Wichita, Omaha and Sioux City.

Pioneer agriculture in Minnesota can be summed up in one word: wheat. By 1878 nearly 70 percent of the state's cultivated land was planted to wheat, and from 1890 to 1900 Minnesota was the top wheat-producing state in the country. Wheat required less soil preparation than most other crops, and there was a ready eastern market for Minnesota wheat, providing farmers with cash payments. The wheat boom also coincided with the advent of steam threshers and the expansion of railroad networks. As settlement pushed westward, the wheat-growing region shifted from southeastern Minnesota to the Red River Valley in the northwest. Capital amassed by growing wheat enabled farmers to diversify, especially into dairy farming. Tremendous wheat yields also fostered a second early Minnesota industry: grain milling.

Stimulated by new technology that greatly improved the quality of flour made from Minnesota's hard spring wheat, the flour milling industry grew quickly, from 81 mills in 1860 to 507 mills 10 years later. "New Process" flour (also known as "Patent" flour because it was made with a patented process), developed at Cadwallader Washburn's Minneapolis mill, made the city this country's leading milling center by 1882, a position it held for almost 40 years. Serving an international market, it sent one third of its output, about 20 percent of U.S. flour exports, to foreign countries. Much of the investment capital and business acumen behind flour milling came from former lumbermen, among them Cadwallader and William D. Washburn, Governor John S. Pillsbury and Dorilus Morrison.

To this day, Minnesota is the nation's leading iron-mining state. When high-grade ore was discovered on the Vermilion Range in the 1880s and the Mesabi a few years later, the rush was on. Thousands of miners and small businessmen thronged the new frontier, raising new towns like Tower, Mountain Iron, Ely, Virginia, Hibbing and Chisholm. Exceeding even its finders' wildest dreams, the Mesabi proved the nation's largest source of iron ore, at one time producing one fourth of the world's iron ore. Iron ore shipments to eastern steel mills also greatly stimulated the expansion of the port of Duluth.

In the 1980s, Minnesota's economic growth, measured in terms of increased employment, is outpacing that of both its Midwestern neighbors and the United States as a whole. While many Minnesota industries still are based on local natural resources—agriculture, food processing, mining, paper manufacturing and tourism—widely-diversified new industries help account for the state's rosy financial outlook. Computer equipment, computer-based business services, printing and publishing, and other professional services are the fastest-growing sectors of the economy.

Agriculture, lumbering and mining still are associated with particular regions of the state, but each has changed drastically. Minnesota is among the top five producers nationally of corn, soybeans, sugar beets, rye, hogs, turkeys, cheese and butter. Wheat remains a primary crop in the Red River Valley, but corn is king state-wide. Primarily a feed crop, corn has stimulated the production of both hogs and beef cattle. This, in turn, has made Minnesota a major meat-packing state. South St.

Logs awaiting shipment at Grand Marais on Lake Superior, Longfellow's "shining Big-Sea Water" in Song of Hiawatha. R. HAMILTON SMITH

Paul has the world's largest livestock market; Austin is the home of the George Hormel Company (which celebrated the 50th anniversary of Spam in 1987).

Predictably, several of Minnesota's top-ranking companies are involved one way or another with food. All of them have expanded in diverse directions, however. The Cargill Company, Minnesota's largest enterprise, is a good example. Founded shortly after the Civil War by Will Cargill with the help of his younger brothers—Sam, Jim and Sylvester—the Cargill Company began with a string of small town grain elevators, and today is the world's biggest grain trader. With annual revenues in the $32 billion dollar range, Cargill's activities include corn milling, soybean processing, meat packing, salt mining, poultry processing and animal feeds, as well as steel and chemical manufacturing and insurance.

General Mills grew out of Cadwallader Washburn's Minneapolis flour mill. Early on, Washburn took John Crosby as his partner, and in the 1920s the Washburn Crosby Company backed WCCO, a fledgling Twin Cities radio station named for the company's initials. Promoting a new Washburn Crosby product named Wheaties, WCCO aired the first singing commercial, set to the tune, "She's A Jazz Baby," on Christmas Eve, 1924. Sixty years ago, General Mills also created America's perennial heroine of the kitchen, Betty Crocker. While continuing to produce and market Gold Medal flour and Wheaties, General Mills is a highly diversified conglomerate primarily concerned with food processing and restaurants.

A second flour-milling giant, the Pillsbury Company, still packages flour and baking products, but it also processes frozen fish, vegetables, pizza and ice cream under such familiar brand names as Pillsbury, Green Giant, Hungry Jack, Totino's, Haagen-Daz and Van de Kamp's. Catering to the eating-out crowd, the Pillsbury Company has 4,743 Burger King restaurants in addition to the Godfather's Pizza, Quik Wok, Bennigan's, Steak and Ale, and Bay Street restaurant chains.

Approaching the food industry from a different angle, Super Valu is the country's largest food wholesaler; it supplies 2,000 retail stores, including more than 100 of its own. The state's fourth-ranking company, Super Valu also owns the County Seat stores, department stores, and insurance, architectural design and interior design firms.

Agriculture and agribusiness will continue to define Minnesota's image, but the state's business character is infinitely more complex. For one thing, there is a glamorous new kid on the block in recent years—the computer industry. Few people realize that the first commercial computer was built in Minnesota. Transforming the 20th-century world in ways that challenge the imagination, computers are the brainchild of Minnesota wizardry. Three of the world's five largest computer manufacturers, Sperry Rand Univac, Honeywell and Control Data are Minnesota companies.

In 1950—working in a building that had been an American Radiator foundry, then a warehouse and finally a glider plant during World War II—William Norris and his colleagues, known collectively as Engineering Research Associates, completed the first general purpose computer system. It was for a National Security Agency facility in Washington, D.C. Four years later, they built the

first computer for commercial use, the ERA 1101. Weighing 16,000 pounds, the ERA 1101 consisted of seven cabinets taking up more than 400 square feet, which housed 2,700 vacuum tubes and miles of electrical wiring.

Remington Rand bought the Norris concern in 1951, offering the computer firm's shareholders a tidy $1.5 million for its assets (a return of 80 to one on their investment). When Remington Rand was subsequently purchased by Sperry Gyroscope in 1955, Norris was named general manager of its computer operations, the Univac Division of Sperry Rand. Two years later, Norris formed his own firm, Control Data, possibly the only corporation ever to go from zero sales to more than $2 billion annually in just 20 years. Employing some of the nation's top technological talent, Honeywell, Univac and Control Data have since spawned dozens of smaller Minnesota computer companies.

The largest of Minnesota's literally thousands of manufacturing firms is 3M (Minnesota Mining and Manufacturing). Five men who knew nothing about mining founded it in 1902, to mine what they thought was a valuable deposit of corundum—but which turned out to be nearly worthless anorthosite. 3M weathered several precarious years before developing a sandpaper that would sell. Many Minnesotans who took a chance on the struggling company in its infancy are millionaires today. Employing 22,000 workers in Minnesota alone, with additional plants in 32 states and 50 foreign countries, 3M is the state's third-largest company, manufacturing thousands of items ranging from 600 kinds of tape to dozens of office machines.

In northeastern Minnesota, iron-ore mining is a changed but still viable business on Minnesota's iron range. While the richest ores mostly have been depleted, in part due to heavy demands during World War II, newly-developed methods of mining lower-grade taconite have revitalized the industry. Currently, eight taconite processing plants established in iron-range communities since the 1950s still produce more than half of the nation's iron ore. Geologists estimate that Minnesota's iron ore reserves will last another 200 years.

Minnesota has 23 billion-dollar businesses, including seven banking and insurance institutions and a transportation titan, Northwest Airlines. Clearly, this is more than its fair share. Minnesota has some 4,150,000 residents, about two percent of the nation's population, and there

are about 550 billion-dollar companies in this country. Given these figures, Minnesota could expect to have 11 or 12 billion-dollar companies; instead it has double that number. From time to time, observers of the state scene have speculated as to possible reasons for Minnesota's superior business profile, and have drawn some interesting conclusions.

The fact that Minnesota is centrally located, making markets throughout the country readily accessible, has

Above: A computer screen reflects the image of a Sperry Rand Univac executive. R. HAMILTON SMITH
Facing page, top: *Twin Cities skylines: St. Paul in foreground is superimposed on cityscape of Minneapolis.* R. HAMILTON SMITH
Bottom: *Warehouse district in Minneapolis.* JOHN STRYKER

MINNESOTA'S TOP TEN COMPANIES
Annual Sales (in billions)

Cargill (grain marketing)	$32.3
Dayton-Hudson (general retailing)	8.8
3M (paper & allied products)	7.8
Super Valu Stores (food wholesaling)	7.5
Honeywell (instruments)	6.6
Pillsbury (food products)	5.1
Control Data (computing equipment)	4.8
General Mills (food products)	4.4
Harvest States Coop (grain marketing)	3.0
St. Paul Companies (insurance)	2.6

THE FALLS OF ST. ANTHONY. *Oil painting by Henry Lewis, 1848-49.* MINNESOTA HISTORICAL SOCIETY

Tilted Thomsonite formation on the St. Louis River in the Arrowhead region.

Facing page: *View from the bluffs above the Mississippi River Valley in southeastern Minnesota.* R. HAMILTON SMITH PHOTOS

THE LEGEND OF ANPETU SAPA

This Dakota story concerns the beautiful Anpetu Sapa (The Dark Day) who took her life and that of her young son at St. Anthony Falls. It was recorded by Mary Eastman, wife of painter Seth Eastman, who was commandant at Fort Snelling in the 1840s. A sacred meeting place for the Dakota, Sacs, Fox and Ojibwe Indians, the falls figured prominently in aboriginal lore.

Young Anpetu Sapa had married a brave and skillful hunter, one she loved beyond measure and who loved her in return, promising to be faithful to her alone. But her husband later broke this pledge, bringing a second wife to their lodge. His stature would surely increase, he thought, and his new marriage allied him to a powerful family. But Anpetu Sapa, the mother of his child, was grieved beyond mending.

One day when the Dakotas were returning from a hunt, laden with deer and buffalo, they reached the portage at St. Anthony Falls. While the others were busy repacking their heavy burdens, Anpetu Sapa took her young son in her arms and paddled to the island in the middle of the river. Dressing in her embroidered bridal garments, with a crown of eagle feathers on her head, she arrayed the little boy as a gallant warrior, putting his tiny bow and arrows in his hand. His father would grieve for him, she knew, but her mother's heart perceived the sad days that lay ahead for the child without its mother.

In the canoe, with the child in front of her where he could best be seen by his father, she paddled toward the falls, singing her death song. On shore, hearing her chant, her husband raced from his new wife's side, running frantically along the bank and calling Anpetu Sapa back. But the sacrifice was done, and the canoe rushed over the precipice, carrying its sad cargo into eternity.

Sometimes, the Indians insisted, Anpetu Sapa's spirit would rise from the white foam, resting lightly on the waters. Holding her infant to her bosom, she looked upon the green prairies where once she lived happily. Then she disappeared.

certainly been a contributing factor. Secondly, Minnesota's invigorating climate is usually mentioned, though I'm not quite sure how this is supposed to spur productivity. Do workers work faster in cold weather trying to keep warm? (It is true that warm humid temperatures in summer tend to slow them down!) I would guess that the Minnesota work ethic is inbred, inherited from no-nonsense Yankee and Scandinavian forefathers. The best reason Minnesota has been lucky in business seems to be that most of its leading firms began in Minnesota, grew in Minnesota, and have chosen to remain in the state.

So why did people come to Minnesota in the first place? The simplest answer to that question is trees. Ironically, Minnesota owes its lively business climate to the very same lumber barons whom history has frequently condemned for stripping the timberlands naked.

The scenario went something like this: The lumbermen cleared the land, the farmer planted wheat, the miller ground the wheat into flour, and these people combined created the need for practical transportation, banking and insurance systems. It was no accident that Minnesota's population figures exploded during the lumber era. Thousands of workers came to cut the trees and man the sawmills, and additional thousands of immigrants came to take up farmsteads. The flour mills needed workers. So did the state's growing network of railroads and many other new businesses. In just 20 years, between 1870 and 1890, Minnesota's population soared from 439,000 to 1.3 million.

How has lumbering fared in the 20th century? The industry reached its peak in Minnesota about 1905, after which the loggers headed for forests in the Pacific Northwest. But the recently discovered potential of trees such as aspen which sprang up in the cutover areas has given the forest products industry in Minnesota new direction.

While the valuable white pine is mostly gone, Minnesota has 16.2 million acres of commercial forest land, more than a quarter of the state's total land area, where aspen, birch, spruce, fir, elm, ash and cottonwood trees are harvested. Most Minnesota timber is used to produce pulpwood for composition lumber products and paper, also cut lumber, Christmas trees, posts, poles and pilings. Because forestry has made giant strides, trees are now considered a crop, and they are replanted as they are cut.

THE LAND

PRECAMBRIAN TIME TO THE PRESENT

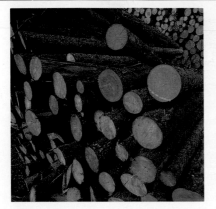

Above: R. HAMILTON SMITH
Right: *Kadunce Creek gorge on North Shore of Lake Superior.*
R. HAMILTON SMITH

Twice in the far distant past, Minnesota had sizable mountain ranges. Spewed up from the earth's seething interior by spectacular volcanism 2,700 million years ago and again about 1,800 million years ago, they long since have eroded, but their roots remain in northern Minnesota and the Minnesota River Valley. (By comparison, the Appalachians are a youthful 225 million years old, and the Rockies, truly adolescent, are only 60 million years old.) Its wild energies thus spent, Minnesota has remained relatively quiet and stable for the past 1,000 million years. No volcanic activity or mountain raising has occurred, and after long years of erosion, chiefly by running water, Minnesota presents a fairly low profile. Situated about equidistant between North America's two main mountain belts, it is near the low-relief center of the continent.

Like all continents, North America has a nucleus or "shield" of old Precambrian rocks, and in Minnesota this shield, called the Canadian Shield, is studied by earth scientists from around the globe. Although heavy glacial debris covers about 99 percent of Minnesota's Precambrian shield, the Lake Superior region features some splendid outcrops, dating from 2,700 million to 600 million years ago. Mute witnesses to eons of earth history, the oldest rocks in this region are the granites and greenstones of the border lakes and iron ranges; the youngest are the basalt lavas, dark gabbros and sandstones of the North Shore.

The Precambrian period, which encompasses seven eighths of the earth's history, is the oldest in geologic time, spanning the years from the origin of the earth, 4,500 million years ago, to the development of invertebrate life, about 600 million years ago. During this time, crustal unrest, wind, water and ice all shaped the face of Minnesota; the earth developed a solid crust, continental seas came and went, mountains were thrust up and destroyed, and glaciers advanced and retreated.

In the southwestern part of the state where the Minnesota River Valley has been deeply eroded, granitic gneisses dating to 3,600 million years ago have been identified. Termed Morton Gneiss (pronounced *nice*) by geologists because it occurs in and near Morton, these outcrops are among the world's oldest rocks, surpassed only by rocks determined to be 3,800 million years old in Greenland and Labrador. Also known as "rainbow rock," Morton Gneiss is a metamorphic, coarse-grained pink, gray and black swirled rock, similar to granite, which is prized as an architectural stone. It is quarried by the Cold Spring Granite Company at Morton and shipped throughout the world.

Minnesota's rich iron formations, which helped make America an industrial giant, also are Precambrian. The Mesabi, Cuyuna and Gunflint Ranges were born of iron-bearing sediment laid down in shallow seas 2,000 million years ago. Nearly all of the world's other major iron formations, in Labrador, Australia, Russia, Venezuela, Brazil and Africa, are about this same age. The still older ores of Minnesota's Vermilion Range, which appear to be volcanic in origin, date to about 2,600 million years ago.

Post-Precambrian time is divided into three eras: Paleozoic (600 million to 225 million years ago), Mesozoic (225 million to 65 million years ago) and Cenozoic (65 million to 2 million years ago). During the Paleozoic era, epic continental seas invaded parts of what is now

Rock climber on North Shore, Lake Superior. TOM TILL

Minnesota, laying down layer upon layer of sedimentary rock, mainly sandstone, dolomite, shale and limestone. These bedded formations, most containing fossils of long-extinct invertebrates, are best seen in southeastern Minnesota, comprising the steep bluffs along the Mississippi River and several of its tributaries. Paleozoic fossils also are found in virtually every road cut and quarry in this region. The most common fossils are bryozoans, similar in appearance to corals; the most spectacular are cephalopods—shelled, squidlike organisms that sometimes attained lengths in excess of 20'.

The Mesozoic Era is known as the age of dinosaurs, which flourished during the Cretaceous period (135 million to 65 million years ago). And while no trace of these reptilian creatures has been found in the state, Minnesota quite likely had its share. In the western states, dinosaur remains are abundant in river, delta and swamp deposits on the edge of the Cretaceous sea that flooded the North American continent. This sea's eastern shore was in western Minnesota. If the kinds of sedimentary deposits that

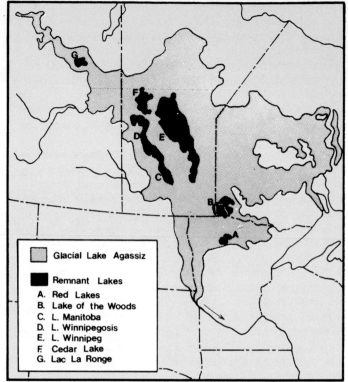

Glacial Lake Agassiz

Remnant Lakes

A. Red Lakes
B. Lake of the Woods
C. L. Manitoba
D. L. Winnipegosis
E. L. Winnipeg
F. Cedar Lake
G. Lac La Ronge

Above: *This boulder, called a glacial erratic, rests where a glacier dropped it.* BOB EIKUM

Right: *The total area eventually covered by the waters of Lake Agassiz. The lake was never this large at any one time. Darker patterns indicate remnant lakes still occupying parts of the basin. (After Elson, 1967.)* FROM *MINNESOTA'S GEOLOGY,* RICHARD W. OJAKANGAS AND CHARLES L. MATSCH, UNIVERSITY OF MINNESOTA PRESS

contain dinosaur bones are present in Minnesota, they are buried under glacial drift. The skull of a Cretaceous marine crocodile was unearthed on the Mesabi Range in 1967, and shark teeth have been found in Cretaceous sediments at open pit sites on the Mesabi Range and in Big Stone County in western Minnesota.

The Minnesota landscape was dry for 200 million years following the advance and retreat of several Paleozoic seas, but about 100 million years ago, warm Cretaceous seas from the north and south advanced into western North America, extending into Minnesota. The climate was subtropical or tropical, and a wide variety of lush vegetation flourished. This warm, moist climate also produced one of Minnesota's outstanding geological features, the high banks of whitish Cretaceous clay that occur along the Redwood River near Redwood Falls. Cretaceous clay is the product of Morton Gneiss decomposed under warm, humid conditions. While not espe-

cially striking in appearance, these clays indicate significant change in Minnesota's climate during the past 100 million years.

By the Cenozoic Era, called the age of mammals, dinosaurs were extinct. How and why they vanished we do not know. The climate cooled and subtropical vegetation disappeared. To the west, the Rocky Mountains rose, and the alluvial material carried down the growing mountains by numerous rivers ultimately formed the Great Plains. The remains of oreodonts (sheeplike mammals) and titanotheres (rhinoceroses), along with numerous other animals, were preserved in these river sediments. Very possibly, these same animals also were present in Minnesota, but this region was too far from the Rocky Mountains to receive the deep accumulations of sediment in which animal remains can fossilize.

During the most recent, and comparatively short, period of geologic time—the Quaternary Period, spanning the last 2 million years—Minnesota's landscape was remodeled to its present appearance, primarily by glacial activity. The mild, stable climate of the Cenozoic Era was replaced by one that fluctuated between warm and cold periods, setting the stage for the Pleistocene Epoch or the Great Ice Age. Between glaciers, the climate moderated, sometimes considerably, with warm interglacial periods lasting hundreds of thousands of years.

Glaciers are actually a simple phenomenon. They occur during long periods of cold weather when more snow falls during the winter than melts in the summer. Ice-Age snow fields sometimes reached depths of several thousand feet, and the weight of the snow compacted the bottom layers into ice. Once a glacier reaches a critical thickness it begins to spread, as one geologist puts it, "like pancake batter in a skillet." Four times during the Ice Age, Minnesota was almost completely covered by south-reaching tongues of the Laurentide Ice Sheet, a massive glacier centered upon what is now Hudson Bay. The last major expansion of glacial ice, called the Wisconsin glaciation, laid the basis for Minnesota's fertile soil and sculpted its thousands of lakes.

As the last glacier pushed southward over hills and valleys, mountains and plains, it scraped off great quantities of rock and soil, carrying along everything from giant boulders to fine dust. Boulders thus embedded in the glacier became abrasives, scarring and often gouging large grooves in the underlying bedrock. This is how the rocky basins of many of Minnesota's northern lakes were carved. Some large boulders known as "erratics" were left standing on the glacial plain. One such erratic is a 20-ton block of greenstone near Montevideo, transported by a glacier from the northern part of the state.

The majority of Minnesota's 12,000-plus lakes formed as the glacier melted, depositing accumulated debris called "drift"—everything from fine clay to boulders—unevenly across the landscape, creating ground moraines or till plains. Many lakes formed in depressions in ground moraines, beginning with the accumulation of meltwater. Still other basins were formed by large chunks of ice left buried or half-buried by the glacier as it retreated. When these huge ice blocks melted, they became lakes.

During periods when the glacier was melting at approximately the same rate that it was advancing, terminal moraines composed of great quantities of unsorted sand,

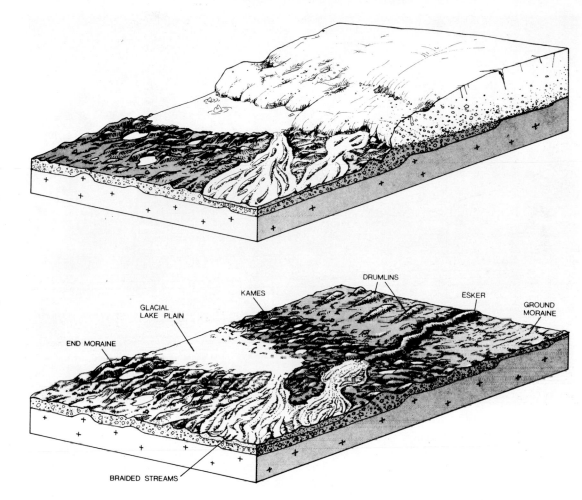

pebbles, clay and boulders formed at its outer edges. The greatest terminal moraine in Minnesota takes the form of a large reverse question mark, beginning at Albert Lea and extending northward to the Twin Cities, westward toward Willmar, northwestward toward Glenwood and Detroit Lakes, eastward toward Park Rapids, and southeastward toward Brainerd. A hummocky, pitted belt, more than 10 miles wide, it rises from less than 50' to as much as 400' above the surrounding glacial plain, containing many irregular hills and basins. Terminal moraines make notoriously poor cropland, having coarse soil, steep hills and poor drainage, but they are exceptionally scenic

These block diagrams portray the various landforms associated with glacier margins. Meltwater produces lakes and braided stream channels. Moraines are built along the margins of glaciers. Eskers are sinuous ridges of sand and gravel marking the former courses of subglacial rivers. Drumlins are streamlined hills formed by actively moving ice. FROM MINNESOTA'S GEOLOGY, RICHARD W. OJAKANGAS AND CHARLES L. MATSCH, UNIVERSITY OF MINNESOTA PRESS

Minnesota farmers probably curse continental glaciation for soils like these in the Detroit Lakes region— they show typical unsorted rocky moraine material. GEORGE WUERTHNER

areas with many lakes. Central Minnesota can thank ground moraines for the high marks it gets from tourists.

The Wisconsin glaciation began about 75,000 years ago, spreading icy fingers across Minnesota during ensuing millennia until its end was decreed by a general warming of the earth's atmosphere about 13,000 years ago. As the glacier receded through northwest Minnesota and North Dakota, it created Glacial Lake Agassiz, the largest freshwater lake ever known on the North American continent. Covering all of northwestern Minnesota, parts of North Dakota and Saskatchewan, and much of Manitoba and Ontario, Glacial Lake Agassiz was larger than all the present Great Lakes combined. Named for Swiss-American geologist Louis Agassiz, who first postulated the Ice Age theory in the 1800s, it was 700 miles long and as much as 700' deep. Combined with Lake Agassiz, numerous smaller glacial lakes helped flood the landscape.

Initially, Lake Agassiz's waters discharged southward, forming the Glacial River Warren, which carved the enormous Minnesota River Valley. As the glacier retreated into Canada, lower-lying channels were uncovered, and Lake Agassiz did a turnabout, draining northward into Hudson Bay. The Red River of the North formed across Lake Agassiz's former lake bed, which became the vast, flat Red River Valley of today, and the great River Warren subsided. Remnants of Glacial Lake Agassiz remain in Red Lake, Lake of the Woods, Lake Winnipeg in Manitoba and hundreds of smaller lakes. The new plumbing system that developed to drain the region included the Mississippi, the Rum, the St. Croix and the Crow rivers.

Vegetation was particularly affected during periods of glaciation. For one thing, tundra conditions in the north forced the tree line to retreat southward. Recent studies indicate that tundra terrain, permanently frozen ground, prevailed in central Minnesota from about 20,000 to 14,000 years ago. In northeastern Minnesota, it persisted a few thousand years longer. In response to warming conditions, plant life reinvaded glaciated areas, establishing prairie and forest landscapes in keeping with climate and topography. Spruce trees flourished in southern Minnesota for at least 3,000 years before birch and alder became the dominant tree types, this change occurring in the Twin Cities area about 11,000 years ago. As the climate grew warmer still, the birch and alder forests were replaced by elm and oak. Eventually, southern Minnesota's hardwood forests gave way to prairie. In the north, jack pine and red pine had established a foothold by 10,000 years ago, and pine has since remained the dominant forest type in that region.

The Ice Age also contributed to the evolution, migration and extinction of numerous animals. As the climate cooled before the last glacier, large animals that lose body heat more slowly, including giant beavers, mastodons, mammoths and bison, flourished in what is now Minnesota. Adapting to climatic conditions, certain animals such as the wooly mammoth and the wooly rhinoceros developed heavy coats. We know from bog deposits in the Great Lakes states that many of these large animals migrated northward as the ice sheets retreated, but none of them survived the Ice Age.

Curiously, beginning about 11,000 years ago, numerous large land animals in North America became extinct—including ground sloths, mammoths, mastodons,

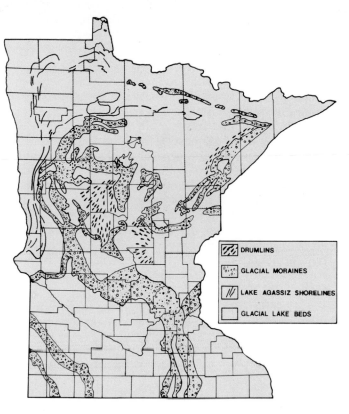

DRUMLINS
GLACIAL MORAINES
LAKE AGASSIZ SHORELINES
GLACIAL LAKE BEDS

llamas, camels, horses, giant armadillos and saber-toothed cats. Their mysterious disappearance remains one of the puzzles of the Ice Age, but it would appear that human predators decimated them. Radiocarbon dating at stampede and fire-drive kill sites in the Great Plains has established the presence of skilled hunters with sophisticated stone weapons between 13,000 and 11,000 years ago. In Minnesota, a site near Lake Itasca has yielded the bones of at least 16 bison that were killed and butchered with stone tools between 8,000 and 7,000 years ago. Quite possibly, Paleo-Indians saw the last glacier retreating toward Canada.

Presenting great diversity in its topographic features, the surface of Minnesota ranges from 602′ above sea level at Lake Superior to 2,301′ above sea level at Eagle Mountain, just 13 miles from the North Shore of Lake Superior. Flat prairies to the west merge with the rolling hills and

lake country of Minnesota's heartland—while the forested rocky ridges that rise north of Lake Superior, remainders of long-ago mountains, contrast sharply with the stream-cut hills in the unglaciated southeast. The climate is hardly uniform, and the vegetation varies considerably.

Minnesota straddles the transition zone between America's eastern woodlands and the western prairies, or more precisely, from the northern coniferous forests to the corn belt of mid-continent. If you were to draw a diagonal line across Minnesota, from the southeastern corner of the state northwestward to North Dakota at the Canadian border, dividing the state into two large triangles, you would have delineated its natural forest and prairie parts. At the time of white settlement, all of the land in the upper right-hand triangle was forested, part of the eastern forest belt that extended from the Atlantic coast to slightly west of the Mississippi. This included both deciduous and conifer forests, with pines predominating roughly east of the Mississippi and north of Pine City.

The deciduous zone bordered the western fringe of the forest belt, forming Minnesota's Great Woods where red, white and burr oak trees, as well as other hardwoods including maple, butternut and black walnut, commonly grew to 100'. Bounded roughly by St. Cloud, Elk River, Mankato and Northfield today, this diagonal area was one of the first to be taken up by farmers. Certain that the region was fertile if it supported such trees, they quickly cleared the land, often burning the timber. The small remaining portion of Minnesota's Great Woods is preserved in Nerstrand State Park near Faribault.

In Minnesota's southwestern triangle, pioneer settlers found themselves engulfed in a tallgrass prairie, dotted with marshes, that stretched from one horizon to the other. Some of the common grasses were big bluestem, little bluestem, Indian grass, prairie clover, goldenrod and pasqueflower. Prairie soils are rich and deep, having developed on thick deposits of glacial till, and these grasslands and accompanying prairie wetlands were prime habitat for countless species of wildlife from buffalo and white wolves to cranes, prairie chickens, shorebirds and waterfowl. Once agriculture became the backbone of the state's economy in the second half of 1800s, 99 percent of the native prairie landscape disappeared under the plow.

Buffalo at Blue Mounds State Park. MINNESOTA TOURISM DIVISION

Until the last precious few of them were killed in the Red River Valley in the late 1800s, large numbers of bison, or buffalo, roamed Minnesota's prairies for many thousands of years. Standing taller, and having longer, straighter horns than buffalo today, the earliest bison provided Minnesota's prehistoric people with food, clothing, shelter and tools. Buffalo bones dating to 7,000 to 9,000 years ago have been found in peat deposits throughout the state, including a kill site at Itasca State Park.

Later hunters stalked the buffalo as it evolved to its modern form, according to evidence in food refuse piles at several prehistoric archaeological sites. Dating from about 200 BC to 500 AD, Laurel culture Indians near International Falls hunted buffalo, as did the ancestors of the Santee Sioux at Mille Lacs Lake and their Oneota neighbors in the Blue Earth Valley. At three sites in west-central Minnesota, buffalo remains have been found in association with human burials.

In the 1930s, one 85'-long burial ground overlooking Lake Traverse was excavated, revealing nine young adult buffaloes buried with human interments. In Pope County, a circular mound contained human burials and that of a single buffalo calf without its head. In a third mound in Ottertail County, inverted buffalo skulls radiating in a circular pattern were unearthed in shallow fill above a central burial pit for humans.

Since only about one percent of Minnesota's once more than 10,000 Indian mounds have been excavated, it can be assumed that there are other buffalo burials as well. The key role played by the buffalo in Indian culture carried over to the grave.

In a state that is 406 miles long north to south, more than a quarter the total distance between Hudson Bay and the Gulf of Mexico, it stands to reason that winters are most severe in the north. You need travel only from southwest to northeast to realize that Minnesota spans the transition zone from the dry, sunny southwest to the cloudier Great Lakes region. The northeast experiences frigid winters, piling up an average of 70″of snow, and its summers are notably cool. In some low-lying areas frost can occur year-round. In the southwest, winter is both drier and shorter, with as little as 40″of snow in some parts, but its warm, sunny summers can be notably dry.

Mark Twain once complained that the coldest winter he ever spent was one summer in Duluth. Any way you look at it, Minnesota's weather likely will never win a popularity contest. But on the other hand, it probably will keep the state from becoming heavily populated. At least to some degree, Minnesotans need to cooperate with the environment in order to survive. Being far from the oceans, Minnesota has a continental climate. Warm in summer, it is cold in the winter, and its temperatures tend to fluctuate widely. The thermometer has registered -59° F in winter, while the summertime temperature has soared to 114° F. Temperatures in

Above: *Remnant of Minnesota's Big Woods at Nerstrand State Park near Faribault.* B.A. FASHINGBAUER
Left: *Hill Anex Mine on Iron Range. Heritage of the earth's heat and pressure at depth is mineralization that has fed the iron-ore industry.* DANIEL J. COX

Minnesota's winters, if not loved, are put to good effect as at St. Paul's Winter Carnival. **Above:** *Ice sculpture has turned into an annual event with many contestants.* **Right:** *Speed-skating event.*
R. HAMILTON SMITH PHOTOS

the cities of Duluth, St. Paul and Moscow are much the same.

Making the most of the "salubrious climate," as they called it, pioneer Minnesotans touted its restorative powers in territorial newspapers, promotional literature and letters back East. Many people (including Dr. William Mayo, who was suffering from malaria) came to Minnesota with high hopes that the weather would cure whatever ailed them. Tuberculosis was a common complaint, and health spas and resorts sprang up. This was the start of Minnesota's tourist industry. When physicians later learned that climate has little to do with conquering disease, resort owners took to soliciting vacationers instead of patients. The weather might not be curative, but it was downright refreshing. Minnesota lakeside resorts became favorite watering holes for well heeled refugees from warmer climes.

If Minnesotans complain about cold winters—and who can blame them?—they also make sport of them. The country's first ski-jumping clubs were organized in Minneapolis and Red Wing in the early 1880s, and Minnesotans, good Scandinavians that many of them are, have been skiing ever since, both downhill and cross-country. It's no accident that Shipstad and Johnson's Ice Follies originated in the Twin Cities; little girls grow up knowing how to figure skate, and boys of all ages play hockey. More Olympic and professional hockey players come from Minnesota than any other state, and Minnesotans invented the snowmobile (much to the displeasure of some environmentalists).

In the 1880s, when a reporter for an eastern newspaper remarked that St. Paul was another Siberia, unfit for human habitation in winter, St. Paulites responded with America's first Winter Carnival, a 10-day cold-weather tribute to Borealis, Ruler of the North Wind. Complete with a bedazzling ice palace in Central Park, the gala featured races on toboggans, skis, snowshoes and skates. Parades with marching bands and extravagant floats were the order of the day, and the reigning royalty included a beautiful snow queen whose escorts wore polar bear costumes. In 1986, celebrating the 100th anniversary of Winter Carnival, St. Paul built the world's tallest ice palace. Millions came to ogle it, and it received press coverage around the globe.

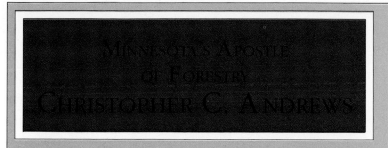

MINNESOTA'S APOSTLE OF FORESTRY
CHRISTOPHER C. ANDREWS

"I had always loved trees," Christopher C. Andrews wrote in his memoirs, published in 1928. Originally from Massachusetts, Andrews was a practicing lawyer who moved to St. Cloud before the Civil War, serving in that conflict as a brigadier general with the Minnesota Volunteers. Later, when he was appointed U.S. minister to Sweden and Norway in 1869, Andrews had the opportunity to study Scandinavian reforesting projects, and he came back to this country urging practical forest planning.

For many years, his proposals fell on deaf ears. The loggers were having their way in the northern forests, and everybody was benefitting— the railroads, timber companies and land speculators, all insisting that lumbermen were only opening the way for farmers. Few people really believed that the immense timberlands ever could be denuded, and conservation was an unpopular subject in Minnesota.

It took a series of forest fires in Pine County in 1894, which claimed 413 lives, to bring home just how vulnerable Minnesota's forests actually were. Year after year, in fact, forest fires were an almost inevitable result of logging. Some fires were accidental, but others were deliberately set to clear cutover land of tree stumps and debris. The year following the Pine County holocaust, Christopher Andrews was named Minnesota's first Chief Fire Warden, charged with directing the activities of more than a thousand local fire wardens.

While Andrews fought fires faithfully, his other duties, and his real mission as he saw it, included investigating "the extent of the forests in the state, together with the amounts and varieties of the wood and timber growing therein…the method used, if any, to promote the regrowth of timber, and any other important facts relating to forest interests." Writing report after report, Andrews pointed out

that forests should occupy only that land unfit for agriculture, that annual cutting never should exceed annual growth, and that timberlands should be constantly renewed by replanting.

Proving Andrews' predictions that Minnesota's pine forests would be virtually exhausted by the early years of this century, Minnesotans were importing lumber from the Pacific Northwest at the time of his death in 1922. At the same time, his gospel of good forestry was beginning to produce results. Due to

Andrews' decades of unflagging advocacy, a School of Forestry was established at the University of Minnesota to promote sound forestry practices, a state nursery was started, and state parks became forest reserves.

In 1911 the legislature approved a bill written by the state forestry board, of which Andrews was secretary, that empowered the board to manage and protect Minnesota forests. Andrews also initiated the movement that resulted in the creation of Minnesota National Forest (la-

ter Chippewa National Forest), in the vicinity of Cass Lake, and the Superior National Forest, north of Lake Superior, comprising more than a million acres of national forest.

Unfortunately, most of Minnesota's forests are vastly changed. Before Yankee lumbermen took to the north woods, 70 percent of Minnesota was timbered. This amount has been reduced to about 34 percent, by both logging and farming, and the remaining forests consist primarily of fast-growing aspen, birch and jack pine trees that sprang up in the cutover areas. Nonetheless, Minnesota's Division of Forestry currently manages 17 million acres of forest in the state, helping make timber processing Minnesota's third-largest manufacturing industry.

THE PEOPLE
INDIANS TO IMMIGRANTS

Above: *Traditional Indian dress at the annual Grand Portage powwow, attended by Ojibwe, Dakota and other Indian people from the U.S. and Canada.* R. HAMILTON SMITH
Right: *Watercolor sketch of a permanent Dakota residence by Seth Eastman, an army officer who served at Fort Snelling in the 1840s.* MINNESOTA HISTORICAL SOCIETY

On June 16, 1931, the operator of a grader digging a road across the former bed of Glacial Lake Pelican in Otter Tail County unearthed a shiny white clam shell 10′ below ground level. Work came to a halt, and highway crew members digging by hand soon discovered a human skull that had been partially crushed by the machine. Two hours later, they had exhumed an almost complete skeleton, a broken tool made of elk antler and a shell pendant. Called "Minnesota Man," the skeleton is actually that of a teen-aged Paleo-Indian girl. Should she be as ancient as the glacial deposits in which she was found, dating to almost 11,000 years ago, she is among North America's oldest known skeletons.

Descended from Asiatic forebears, Minnesota's Paleo-Indians were nomadic big game hunters who moved into the region as the glaciers retreated. Known by their distinctive fluted projectile points (called Clovis and Folsom points for sites in New Mexico), they hunted tusked mammoths and giant bison. Archaeological evidence suggests that these people lived on game and fish, gathering wild rice, fruits, berries and nuts. Although no dwelling sites for Paleo-Indians are known in Minnesota, their projectile points have surfaced in western Minnesota, usually in plowed fields and along gullies and riverbanks.

In northern Minnesota, dating to between about 500 BC and 1000 AD, the Grand Mound on the Rainy River is the largest prehistoric Indian burial mound in the Upper Mississippi region. More than 100' in diameter, nearly that wide, and more than 40' high, it was built by Laurel culture Indians who may have been cannibals.

The Grand Mound itself remains unexcavated (although it was tunneled early in this century by pot hunters reaching the site on excursion steamboats from International Falls, and Port Francis, Ontario, who were literally handed shovels to see what they could find). A smaller mound at the site was examined in 1933 by Minnesota archaeologist Albert E. Jenks, who unearthed the skeletal remains of more than 100 people, layered in four tiers of secondary burial bundles. Many of the bones had been broken to remove the marrow, and skulls had holes drilled in them to extract the brains. Jenks also found primary burials near the surface of the mound, believed to belong to a later culture. At the turn of the century, Minnesota had an estimated 10,000 burial mounds, some of them effigy mounds in the shape of birds, buffaloes, bears and snakes. Unfortunately, due to farming, road building and general carelessness, only a fraction of them still exist. Although built by earlier cultures, some of these mounds apparently were used over a long span of time by later prehistoric Indians as well as Indians of the historic period, including the Dakota. This is the case in St. Paul where six mounds on a high bluff overlooking the Mississippi are preserved in Indian Mounds Park.

According to explorer Jonathan Carver, who visited the area in 1766, the St. Paul mounds then covered the entire bluff. It was "the burying-place of several bands of the [Dakota] Indians: though these people have no fixed residence, living in tents, and abiding but a few months on one spot, yet they always bring the bones of their dead to this place." When several of the mounds were excavated in the late 1880s, they yielded numerous artifacts nearly 2,000 years old. One unusual find was a

The still-unexcavated Grand Mound—a prehistoric Indian burial mound—at Rainy River.
R. HAMILTON SMITH

Left: *Indian petroglyphs at Hegman Lake in Boundary Waters Canoe Area.* STEVEN C. KAUFMAN

27

Indian graves, presumably Dakota, at the mouth of the Minnesota River. Watercolor by Seth Eastman, 1847.
MINNESOTA HISTORICAL SOCIETY

skull encased in red clay. When the funeral mask was removed, the skull was determined to be that of a five-year-old child.

Most of the Indian mounds that have been excavated in Minnesota contain "primary" and "secondary" burials. In primary burials, the entire body is interred, often in an upright, sitting position, with the knees drawn up and the head resting on them. Grave goods including tools and ornaments commonly accompany this type of burial. Secondary burials consist of bundles of bones, the partial remains of bodies that have decomposed in the open (on scaffolds or tied in trees), or that have been buried in shallow graves and later exhumed. Secondary burials are the most numerous in Minnesota mounds; usually they lack grave goods.

When the first Europeans reached Minnesota, it was occupied by Dakota (or Sioux) and Ojibwe (or Chippewa) Indians. Dakota means allies, referring to these Indians' seven tribal groups, while the term "Sioux" originated as a French corruption (Nadouessioux) of an

Ojibwe word meaning snake or enemy. Chippewa is a corruption of "Ojibwe," which may be a form of *o-jib-o-weg,* meaning "those who make pictographs." For several centuries, Ojibwe priests preserved their people's history and knowledge of medicine in symbols on birchbark rolls. Neighboring tribes called them Ojibwe, but these Indians are known in their own language as Anishinabe meaning "original or first people."

The Dakota people once occupied much of what is now Minnesota, with a large center at and around Mille Lacs Lake, but by 1800 they had been driven out of the northern forests, pushed south and west onto prairie lands by westward-moving Ojibwe from the Sault Ste. Marie region who had obtained firearms from French traders. From that time, the two tribes remained perpetual enemies, and their constant warring hindered both the fur trade in the area and, later, white settlement.

Living in bark-covered lodges in summer villages along the banks of the Mississippi and Minnesota rivers, the Dakota were hunters and gatherers who tended small garden plots of corn, their lives following an annual cycle. Once their corn was harvested in the fall, the women left the village to gather wild rice and the men to hunt muskrats—trapping, shooting or spearing the animals. (The Indians ate the muskrat meat while the traders got the skins.) In October the tribes abandoned their villages to hunt deer and other game through the winter, living in easily-transported cone-shaped skin tipis. In January, if the hunt had been successful, the Indians returned to their villages or set up their tipis in a sheltered spot to await spring, living on venison and corn. Springtime meant maple sugaring and renewed muskrat hunting. In summer, the people hunted small game and waterfowl, fished and collected berries and tubers.

In the northern forests, the Ojibwe had brought firearms, iron and brass kettles, trade blankets, and iron and steel tools west with them. They live in dome-shaped wigwams made of birch bark, and they traveled the waters in birchbark canoes. Their culture and language differed from those of the Dakota, but their subsistence lifestyle was remarkably similar. They also hunted, fished and harvested wild food in season, gathering maple sugar in the spring and wild rice in the fall. Besides corn, they planted potatoes, beans, pumpkins and squash. While the Dakota placed their deceased kin on scaffolds, the Ojibwe buried their dead.

Warring was a way of life for both tribes, with scalping a standard procedure, but the Indians also were gregarious persons, fond of decorating their bodies with paint and feathers, who loved feasts, games and betting. They put great stock in the supernatural, and expressed their religious beliefs in songs, dances and elaborate rituals. The Dakota and Ojibwe also possessed a rich oral tradition of stories and legends, much of which has been transcribed in historic times.

Minnesota's Indian heritage is remembered in the state's many Dakota and Ojibwe place names. The southern Minnesota cities of Wabasha, Shakopee, Red Wing and Sleepy Eye are constant reminders of prominent Dakota chiefs, while Winona recalls the heroine who leaped to her death from a Mississippi River bluff rather than marry a man she didn't love. Eight southern Minnesota counties bear practical Dakota names: Anoka ("on both sides"), Dakota ("alliance" or "league"), Isanti (the former name of a large division of the Dakota now called Santees), Kandiyohi ("where the buffalo fish come"), Wabasha ("red leaf"), Waseca ("rich," especially in provisions), Watonwan ("where fish bait abounds") and Winona ("first-born daughter").

Counties in northern Minnesota with Ojibwe names include Chisago ("large, lovely lake"), Kanabec ("snake"), Koochiching ("neighbor lake and river," referring to Rainy Lake and the Rainy River), Mahnomen ("wild rice") and Wadena ("a little round hill"). That the Indians also had a sense of humor is apparent in the Ojibwe word for one of Minnesota's largest lakes: Winnibigoshish means "miserable wretched dirty water."

The first white man known certainly to have reached Minnesota was French explorer Daniel Greysolon, Sieur Duluth, for whom Minnesota's international port city is named. Sponsored by a company of Montreal and Quebec fur merchants, Duluth's party paddled west from Montreal through the Great Lakes, rendezvousing with the Dakota near where the city of Duluth now stands. Accompanying the Indians inland to their principal village on the south shore of Mille Lacs Lake, Duluth formally claimed the north country by right of discovery for his monarch, Louis XIV, on July 2, 1679.

Like the British who came after them, the French dared hope to find the fabled Northwest Passage to China, but they settled gladly for a wealth in furs. Occupying the northern wilderness for the next century, French fur

MOCCASIN FLOWER

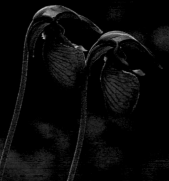

Moccasin flower, or pink lady's slipper. D. CAVAGNARO

According to Ojibwe legend, long ago in the northern forest, there once lived a young man and his beautiful sister. The maiden longed to accompany her brother on his hunting trips, but he always refused her, sending her back to the wigwam. One day as her brother set out, not wanting to be disappointed again, the girl followed, keeping far enough behind him so as not to be seen.

Once deep in the woods, the maiden became lost and was unable to find either her brother or the way back to her village. When her brother returned from hunting and found his sister missing, the villagers began a search for the girl. Starting a fire, they sent up smoke signals to her, but a strong wind whipped the fire out of control and the forest fire that ensued consumed the maiden.

When the next spring came, the Indians watched a beautiful new flower spring up, one they had never seen before. Pink and white, it was shaped like a moccasin, and the flowers led into the woods. Following their path, the Indians found the remains of the missing maiden. Wherever she had stepped, a flower had grown. To this day, the flowers continue growing.

The moccasin flower, sometimes called the lady's slipper, is Minnesota's state flower. A showy pink-and-white orchid-like flower, its botanical name, *cypripedium*, derives from Greek words meaning "shoe of Venus." Found in every part of the state, it grows best in cool and moist woods and in bogs.

Ojibwe burial ground at Leech Lake. B.A. FASHINGBAUER

men built several posts in what became Minnesota, pioneering the trade in beaver skins and other furs. Opening new routes to the American West, they explored mid-America, creating a legacy of maps. After the final French and Indian War in 1763, the French formally relinquished their claims in the New World to England, but their presence remains in numerous Minnesota place names, including Mille Lacs, Faribault, Hennepin, Le Sueur and Grand Marais.

The British built dozens of fur posts in Minnesota, dominating the region until after the War of 1812 (which was fought in part to oust them from territory belonging to the newly-formed United States), but Frenchmen remained integral to their operations. English and Scottish proprietors with headquarters in Canada might control the company purses, but they employed seasoned French and mixed-blood traders who continued to act as intermediaries with the Indians. Three great British firms, sometimes in bitter conflict with each other, operated in Minnesota: the Hudson's Bay Company, the North West Company and the XY Company. Near Pine City on the Snake River, the Minnesota Historical Society staffs a reconstructed six-room North West Company wintering post dating from 1804.

With similar goals and activities, the French and British eras in the Northwest were much alike, at least as far as the Indians were concerned. Both countries limited their designs to mapping new commercial routes and conducting profitable trade with the Indians. If they considered colonizing the north country, they did not do so, and they posed little threat to the Indians' traditional way of life. Once the American flag was raised in this part of the world, however, the plot took a new turn. The United States began mapping and enforcing permanent boundaries to protect its newly-won fur trade, but its more pressing concern was dictated by Manifest Destiny.

Following the Louisiana Purchase, Lieutenant Zebulon Pike was dispatched upriver from St. Louis in 1805 to locate a site on which to build a military fort and a government trading house. Arriving at the confluence of the Mississippi and the Minnesota rivers, Pike concluded an agreement with the Dakota, assuring them a suitable price to be decided by Congress, and paying them $200 in trade goods and 60 gallons of liquor on the spot, for an area that included most of present-day Minneapolis and St. Paul. Fourteen years later, Congress approved the

niggardly sum of $2,000 to settle this account. The trading post that might have benefitted the Indians never materialized, but in August 1819 troops of the Fifth Infantry arrived at the junction of the two rivers to build the promised military post.

Named for its first commanding officer, Fort Snelling was the first and finest fort in the American West. Built of native limestone on top precipitous 100' bluffs, it was a diamond-shaped citadel, reminiscent of a medieval fortress. Buff-colored stone walls, 10' high and three feet thick, contained this self-sufficient military outpost, and its solid construction and strategic position rendered it virtually impregnable. At the east end of the 600'-long parade ground, Colonel Josiah Snelling's personal square-built limestone residence, Georgian in spirit but faced with a flamboyant Flemish gable, was a jewel on the frontier.

Fort Snelling was manned by up to two dozen officers, most of them graduates of West Point, and as many as 300 enlisted men, a good number of whom were European immigrants. Its stables could quarter 100 horses. A four-story commissary carved into the perpendicular riverbank stored four years' provisions and supplies. The nation's northwesternmost outpost from 1819 until 1849, Fort Snelling secured American fur interests in the area and maintained an uneasy peace between the Dakota and Ojibwe Indians, preparing the way for white settlement.

Minnesota's first school was organized within the walls of Fort Snelling, as were its first hospital, circulating library, brass band and Protestant congregation. In 1823 the first steamboat to reach the post, the *Virginia,* brought an Italian nobleman, Count Giacomo Beltrami, one of numerous explorers, missionaries and travelers who enjoyed the fort's hospitality. Beltrami had come to

Above: FORT SNELLING. *Oil painting by Henry Lewis, ca. 1850.*
MINNESOTA HISTORICAL SOCIETY
Left: *A costumed interpretive guide at the reconstructed Fort Snelling.*
R. HAMILTON SMITH

Facing page: *An Ojibwe man raises the American flag at Grand Portage National Monument, an important early fur-post site.* R. HAMILTON SMITH

was, in fact, no price Wanata would accept for his prize. Beltrami implored Snelling's wife, Abigail, to intercede, and she made a valiant try. Wanata patiently heard her out, then told her that if she would cut off her floor-length black hair and braid it for him to wear it in its place, he would give up the necklace. End of negotiations.

Beginning a multi-million dollar restoration project in the 1960s, the Minnesota Historical Society has restored Fort Snelling to its former glory. Few of the fort's current structures are the originals, but they have been faithfully replicated in newly-quarried limestone. The Historical Society's interpretive staff, costumed as soldiers and their womenfolk, whisk visitors back in time 160 years. The year is 1827, and as yet there is no non-military white settlement in Minnesota. Fort Snelling is the seat of power in this northern domain; its officers, the ruling aristocracy.

Opposite Fort Snelling, on the east bank of the Mississippi, Mendota (a Dakota word meaning "meeting of the waters") is the oldest permanent white settlement in Minnesota. Because of its fortunate location at the junction of two rivers, French Canadian fur traders frequented this area as early as the late 1770s. After permanent trading camps were established there in the 1820s, Mendota became one of Minnesota's most important fur-trade centers. Much of the credit belongs to Henry Hastings Sibley. Twenty-three years old when he arrived on horseback at this outpost in 1834, Sibley was bent on making it the capital of his fur-trade empire.

The well-educated son of a pioneer Michigan judge, Sibley was the newly-appointed head of the American Fur Company's Sioux outfit, which took in most of the present states of Minnesota, North and South Dakota and the Canadian province of Saskatchewan. The handsome two-story limestone house and fur trade headquarters he built with the help of local Dakota men and women is Minnesota's oldest residence. For the next few years, Indians and traders by the hundreds converged on the post, their oxcarts and canoes piled high with pelts destined for New York and Europe. During his first year in Mendota, Sibley collected 389,000 muskrat skins worth $44,000 (beaver skins were scarce by then, with "rat" skins replacing them as the usual medium of trade), and numerous mink, deer, beaver, raccoon, otter, martin, bear, fox, wolf, badger, wildcat and rabbit pelts. He also noted 1,000 buffalo robes.

Stockade at Grand Portage on Lake Superior's North Shore.
R. HAMILTON SMITH

America to find the true source of the Mississippi, and he would go home thinking he had done just this, imagining himself in the company of such earlier Italian explorers as Marco Polo and Christopher Columbus. In reality, the small, heart-shaped lake he found and named Lake Julia actually empties into the Red River basin.

Remaining several weeks with Snelling and his family, Beltrami was also collecting Indian curios to take back to Italy. He managed to talk one of the young Snelling children out of an elkhorn bow and quiver of 24 arrows that it might "grace the halls of ancient Rome," but he had less luck in wangling a necklace of bears' claws he coveted from a Dakota man named Wanata. There

In 1839 a Dakota woman named Red Blanket Woman gave birth to Sibley's daughter, Helen Hastings. Both mother and child were allowed to fade quickly into historical obscurity, but there is a record of the girl's attending classes at an early mission school for mixed-blood children, most of whose fathers were officers at Fort Snelling. Subsequently, Sibley married Sarah Steele from Baltimore, the sister of the sutler at Fort Snelling, who turned his fur trade headquarters into a proper residence, covering the rough walls with flowered paper, and ordering a Brussels rug and a piano from New York. Seven of the Sibleys' nine children were born in the house.

Mendota prospered under Sibley, but its heyday was brief. By the 1840s, the end of the fur trade already was evident. Sibley liquidated his fur company assets, investing his money in land and railroads, and involved himself in territorial politics. When Minnesota was admitted to statehood in 1858, Sibley was elected its first governor, the limestone house in Mendota becoming the governor's mansion. Four years later, named commander of Minnesota's volunteer forces during the Dakota War, Sibley moved his family to St. Paul. He sold the house to the Catholic church, which operated a parochial school there for several years. Later, the residence was allowed to deteriorate, almost beyond repair. At its worst, it was a derelict, harboring tramps. The Daughters of the American Revolution restored the Sibley House in 1910, and it now is open to the public during the summer.

In this century, Mendota is famous as a haven for jazz musicians. It all started in 1939 at a roadhouse called Mitch's, where piano player Red Dougherty put together a five-man Dixieland band. Mendota was suddenly on the musical map. Stars like Mel Torme and Peggy Lee were lured to Mendota for guest appearances. When they were playing clubs in the Twin Cities, Hoagy Carmichael, Jack Teagarden, Gene Krupa and Harry James commonly turned up at Mitch's to jam until four or five in the morning. The end came for Mitch's in 1950 when the state took the building for highway construction. These days you can hear the sweetest Dixieland north of New Orleans at Mendota's Emporium of Jazz. The Hall Brothers Jazz Band are the resident musicians, and the show goes on every Friday and Saturday night.

On July 27, 1837, prompted by eastern lumber interests, the United States government negotiated a treaty with the Ojibwe at Fort Snelling for the sale of Indian

Above: A young participant at Rendezvous Days, Pine City.
Left top: Mock Voyageurs' Rendezvous at Fort Snelling State Park.
Left: Fur Trade Rendezvous reenacted on the Snake River at Pine City. R. HAMILTON SMITH PHOTOS

lands along the northern St. Croix. Precisely two months later, Dakota representatives from Minnesota, brought to Washington by Indian agent Lawrence Taliaferro, put their marks on a similar treaty, ceding their rights along the southern portion of the river. When Congress ratified the agreements the next year, the pine-covered delta between the St. Croix and the Mississippi passed to white ownership.

In exchange for the lands, both treaties promised generous annuities in the form of money, goods, provisions and services. But the St. Croix Valley was only the opening wedge, and subsequent treaties, some of them notoriously less fair, quickly consumed the Indians' Minnesota homelands. Minnesota's Indians have suffered enormous degradation and ill treatment at the hands of

STILLWATER

Above: *Built on the comely banks of St. Croix Lake, Stillwater is a pioneer lumber town turned tourist mecca.*
R. HAMILTON SMITH

Left: *Excursion boat waits out winter at Stillwater marina.*
CHARLES J. JOHNSTON

Stillwater bills itself as "the birthplace of Minnesota." While the state's first white settlement occurred in Mendota, this claim is nonetheless valid. The convention of 61 pioneer delegates that sent Henry Sibley to Washington (at his own expense) to petition Congress for territorial status took place in Stillwater in 1848.

Once the 1837 treaties with the Dakota and Ojibwe for the sale of the pine-covered delta between the St. Croix and Mississippi rivers were ratified by Congress, the timberlands were temporarily annexed to Wisconsin Territory. But when Wisconsin was admitted to the Union in 1848, its western boundary was fixed at the St. Croix, leaving soon-to-be Minnesotans outside the pale, so to speak. In Washington, with help from Senator Stephen Douglas, Sibley saw his bill approved by both the Senate and the House; Minnesota Territory was formally organized in 1849.

Stillwater already had been in the lumber business by 1843, its first sawmill built on the banks of Lake St. Croix by four young Yankees. A dozen years later, by the mid-1850s, the town was the boisterous queen of lumbering on the St. Croix. Lumber companies backed by eastern capital purchased enormous tracts of pine lands for $1.25 an acre, hired their own logging crews, and operated sawmills and lumber yards. Much of their prodigious output was sold downstream in Iowa, Illinois and Missouri.

In the years following the Civil War, young Stillwater came of age in the most lavish attire lumbermen could afford; men who made their money cutting and marketing timber flaunted it in their homes. Stillwater is a veritable museum of the delightful distractions of 19th-century architecture. Heavily bracketed squat Italian villas went up next to tall, white pine Gothic houses fairly dripping with medieval trimmings. Circumspect hip-roofed Federal homes were overshadowed by grandiloquent French imperial styles with more fashionable mansard roofs. Downtown, ornate brick and stone business blocks replaced earlier wooden frame structures.

Few people had seen the inevitable. The supply of choice timber and the demand for it were unlimited, most thought, but it took burly loggers little more than 50 years to strip the centuries-old pine forests. By the turn of the century, lumbermen had their sights on the Pacific Northwest. Stillwater's population—which had peaked at 18,000—dwindled to less than half that by 1930, and the town was left choking on its own sawdust.

Recent years have seen a turnabout in Stillwater's fortunes. After decades as a wallflower, this lumberman's mistress is making the most of a second chance. With improved highway access, Stillwater has become a commuters' haven, half an hour from the Twin Cities. Cashing in on her gaudy past, the town also is in the midst of a new boom, this time with tourists who come to ogle the Victorian pretensions.

Preservation is a popular platform. One public-action group saved Stillwater's county courthouse, the oldest in the state, converting it into a center for the arts. Private investors have gambled heavily on renewal, renovating vintage residential and commercial property. Classic church and school buildings have been converted to condominiums. On the riverfront, once crowded with sawmills and lumberyards, pleasure craft vie for marina space.

This much is certain. King Pine once paid Stillwater's way, and his legacy does so still.

whites. Following the Dakota War in 1862, the Dakota people were summarily ousted entirely from the state.

What is somewhat surprising is that Minnesota's Indian population has approximately doubled since the first white men visited the Upper Mississippi Valley. About a quarter of Minnesota's 45,000 Indians live on the state's seven Ojibwe reservations and in four Dakota communities, but the majority of them have gravitated to cities. The Twin Cities has the nation's third-largest urban concentration of native Americans.

Once in American hands, Minnesota in its formative years was shaped by hard-working New England Yankees, most of them descended from families with roots in the British Isles. With high hopes of building a New England in the Northwest, lumbermen from Maine, Vermont and New Hampshire came to fell the trees and stayed to build cities. Puritan ethics stamping their every enterprise, Yankee entrepreneurs founded Minnesota's industries, guided its politics, and organized schools and churches. Several white-painted New England villages pay tribute to their lofty intentions, Marine-on-St. Croix being a good example, but circumstances including the financial panic of 1857 and the Civil War combined to dampen their dreams.

One historian suggests that Minnesota became a New Scandinavia instead. Thousands upon thousands of European immigrants poured into Minnesota during the second half of the 19th century. Germans, Swedes and Norwegians, in that order, comprised the state's largest ethnic groups, but if the Swedes and the Norwegians are counted together, Scandinavians outnumbered Germans.

German families were settling southeastern Minnesota in the 1850s, their prosperous farms soon dotting both the Mississippi and Minnesota river valleys. Swedish immigrants began early farming communities in the St. Croix Valley, where many of the men also worked in the lumber camps. Norwegian settlers took up claims in the lower Mississippi Valley, then spread west and northwest throughout Minnesota to the Red River Valley where they remain the predominant ethnic group. Many Irish also came to Minnesota following the disastrous potato famines in their homeland in the late 1840s, making their presence felt especially in St. Paul. In smaller numbers, French Canadians, Czechs, Dutch, Flemish, Polish, Danish, Welsh, Swiss and Luxemburgers all added to Minnesota's rural mix before 1890.

On the west side of St. Anthony Falls, Minneapolis was a thriving sawmill town by 1860.
MINNESOTA HISTORICAL SOCIETY

Early immigrants traveled several water and overland routes to reach Minnesota, but once the railroad reached the Mississippi River at Galena, Illinois, in 1853, southeastern Minnesota filled rapidly. During the summer navigation season, two boats a day, with as many as 800 passengers, steamed upriver from Galena to Minnesota ports including Winona, Wabasha, Red Wing and St. Paul. In fair weather the trip to St. Paul usually took about three days. Within the state, tributary streams including the Minnesota, the Root and the St. Croix rivers helped transport settlers to their destinations.

Following the Civil War, rail travel made steamboats a thing of the past and changed settlement patterns. Advancing rapidly across the state from centers in Duluth and the Twin Cities, the railroads (there were 15 of them

Stacked on the Stillwater waterfront in 1904, these logs arrived in northern Minnesota by rail from Virginia. They were made into rafts and floated to downriver sawmills on the Mississippi. JOHN RUNK PHOTO; MINNESOTA HISTORICAL SOCIETY

in Minnesota by 1872) partially financed their operations by selling land grants along their trackage. Promoting inland settlement, railroad brochures touting Minnesota's advantages were printed in English, German and the Scandinavian languages, and distributed both in the eastern United States and abroad. Where newcomers had formerly built towns along rivers, primarily in southern Minnesota, their new trade centers went up beside the rail lines throughout the state.

Between 1890 and 1920, immigrants from western and northern Europe continued to pour into Minnesota, but ever more came from southern, central and eastern Europe, including many people from the Russian and Austro-Hungarian empires and smaller numbers from Italy and Greece. By this time, Minnesota's agricultural frontier was nearly closed, and many workers found employment in growing Minnesota industries in cities and on the Iron Range. The Mesabi Range needed thousands of unskilled workers to extract iron ore from its yawning pits, and range towns like Virginia, Hibbing and Chisholm filled with Finns, Ukrainians, Yugoslavians, Italians, Bulgarians, Poles, Hungarians and many others.

Fully 98 percent of Minnesota's 4 million people spring from European stock. The remaining two percent are primarily black, Indian and Mexican-American. There were free black traders in Minnesota during the British era, and a number of black slaves were brought to Minnesota by officers at Fort Snelling. Virginia-born Indian agent Lawrence Taliaferro refers to his slaves in his journals as "servants." (The Indians called them "black Frenchmen.") Taliaferro gave one of his servants, Harriet Robinson, in marriage to Dred Scott at Fort Snelling, performing the ceremony himself, and later emancipated all his slaves. In the 1850s, Dred Scott based his bid for freedom on the fact of his earlier residence in free territory at Fort Snelling.

Other blacks came to St. Paul as steamboat laborers during the Civil War, but the largest numbers came to Minnesota during the southern exodus following World War II. While black Americans comprise more than 11 percent of the national total, they account for less than one percent of Minnesota's population. In the 1980s, Minnesota's 35,000 blacks lived primarily in urban areas, more than 90 percent in three Twin Cities neighborhoods.

Minnesota's largest minority are Spanish-speaking Mexicans and Mexican-Americans. Coming to Minnesota originally as migrant farm workers following World War II, they now number about 50,000, living primarily in the Twin Cities metropolitan area. (In West St. Paul, one family has started a piñata factory.) There are also people of Chinese, Japanese and Filipino ancestry in Minnesota, mostly in the Twin Cities area. Minneapolis and St. Paul have had Korean immigrants since 1965 and, more recently, Southeast Asian refugees arrived by the thousands from 1979 to 1981. The Twin Cities has the nation's second-largest Hmong population, 11,000 people, a figure topped only by California.

A testimony to changing times, today's immigrants arrive by plane. The oldest and second-oldest air carriers in the United States, Western Airlines and Northwest Airlines have been operating out of the Twin Cities since 1926. (Western was purchased by Delta in 1987.) Currently, 28 commercial and commuter carriers serve the Twin Cities International Airport, and a network of more than 150 municipal and private airports and 16 seaplane bases, all of them open to the public, make virtually any point in Minnesota accessible by air.

Empire builder James J. Hill is a larger-than-life figure in Minnesota history, a self-made giant who lured possibly more settlers to the American West than any other man. Born in what is now Ontario, Canada, to immigrant Protestant Irish parents, young Hill was 17 when he left home in 1856, heading for the Orient to seek his fortune. Getting only as far as St. Paul, then in the midst of its first boom, he took a job clerking for a line of packet steamers on the city's waterfront. Jim Hill shipped the first export of Minnesota-grown wheat downriver to St. Louis in 1857; shortly afterwards, he handled the first shipment of Minnesota flour for eastern markets, cutting the stencil to label the barrels himself.

After 20 years' apprenticeship in transportation and related businesses, during which time he put his own line of steamers on the Red River, Hill began what he called the "great adventure" of his life. Buying a nearly bankrupt St. Paul railroad with four other investors, Hill quickly made a financial success of it, personally directing the construction crews that laid rails across western Minnesota, then north to the Canadian border. What had been a trickle of immigrants reaching the Red River Valley became a flood, with Hill's agents in Scandinavian countries recruiting Norwegian and Swedish settlers. Homesteads were free, and Hill was selling railroad lands for $2.50 an acre.

By 1893 Hill's Great Northern Railroad reached Puget Sound, and Hill was offering colonists from eastern states cheap one-way fares west to Montana, Idaho and Washington. In one case, however, his campaign to populate the desolate landscape between Minnesota and the Cascades proved too successful. By the early 1920s, responding to Hill's publicity efforts, homesteaders had settled nearly half of Montana, plowing up the short grass country. Erosion followed, topsoil was blown away, and abandoned farmsteads became commonplace.

To his credit, Hill had an intense interest in farming, which he pursued as a life-long hobby at North Oaks, his 3,000-acre model farm on the outskirts of St. Paul. In the 1880s he was preoccupied with livestock. Grain prices were depressed at a time when he needed to see the area along the Great Northern prosper, and Minnesota and Dakota farmers would be well advised to plant some of their acreage to fodder instead of wheat, he decided. Importing Black Angus beef cattle and shorthorn dairy cattle from Scotland, Hill gave blooded bulls to farmers along his line to build up their herds. A recipient need only promise to care for the animal and service his neighbors' cows for a dollar apiece.

James J. Hill and his son, Louis Hill, Sr. MINNESOTA HISTORICAL SOCIETY

Hill's son and heir, Louis, was largely responsible for Glacier National Park, which, not coincidentally, borders the Great Northern's tracks. In an era when an alpine vacation meant having both time and money for a European holiday, Louis Hill took his idea for a tourist haven in the western wilderness to Washington. Having recently succeeded his father as president of the Great Northern Railroad, he pledged the railroad's considerable resources to the project. Hill's lobbying paid off when Congress established Glacier National Park in 1910.

It is estimated that for every dollar the government spent at Glacier in its first five years, Louis Hill spent $10. The warm bodies of vacationers meant cold cash to the railroad, which until now had relied on freight shipments of timber, minerals and agricultural products. With President Taft's signature barely dry on the bill, Hill had his engineers at Glacier, laying out roads and constructing a string of lodges patterned after Swiss chalets. Hill's first and finest hotel, Glacier Park Lodge, its three-story lobby's balconies supported by 50′ Douglas firs, which Hill had shipped from Oregon and Washington because the government wouldn't let him cut such trees in the park, was up and running in time for the 1913 summer season.

Thanks to Louis Hill, a summer vacation at Glacier National Park became part of the American dream. But it was all part of his father's larger dream. At the time of his death at his red stone Summit Avenue mansion in St. Paul in 1916, James J. Hill could claim a business empire that stretched from the Great Lakes to Washington and Oregon, and from the Canadian border to Missouri and Colorado. Few men in American history have had so great an influence on so vast a territory.

THE TWIN CITIES

MODELS FOR URBAN AMERICA

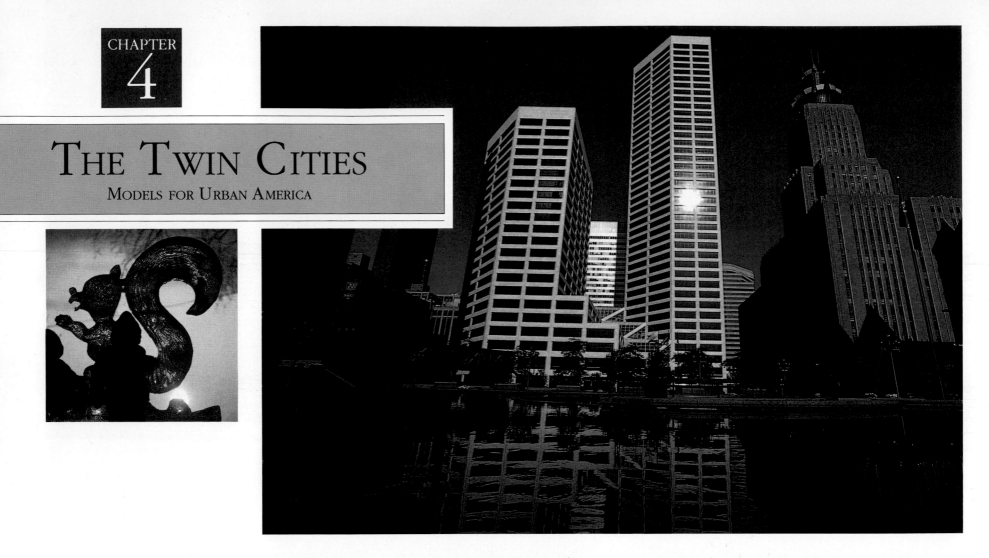

Above: St. Paul Winter Carnival ice sculpture. ***Right:*** The Pillsbury Center in Minneapolis.
Facing page: Reflecting turn-of-the-century style, St. Paul's Capitol is a beaux arts tribute to the glories of ancient Rome. It is seen here during the Fourth of July fireworks that highlight the annual Taste of Minnesota festival. R. HAMILTON SMITH PHOTOS

Identical twins these cities are not. Both claim the Mississippi as their mother, but the river that divides them also defines their orientation.

On the east bank, St. Paul is reminiscent of a city like Boston, steeped in Victorian-era tradition—while Minneapolis, growing up west of the Mississippi, is a vigorous young upstart that has outstripped its older sibling. St. Paul has the state capitol, but Minneapolis's 57-story Investors Diversified (IDS) Tower is the tallest tribute to trade between Chicago and the Pacific Ocean.

Built like Rome on seven hills, St. Paul is a predominantly Catholic city with an Irish image (though more of its immigrants were German). Meantime, Minneapolis, known for its lakes and parks (there are 22 lakes in the city), is heavily Lutheran and plays up its Scandinavian heritage. As Garrison Keillor once explained it, the difference between St. Paul and Minneapolis "is the difference between pumpernickel and Wonder Bread."

Home to 2 million people, half of Minnesota's population, the Twin Cities metropolitan area is the cultural and commercial capital of the Upper Midwest. Not infrequently, both cities appear at the top of polls measuring quality of life, the indicators being housing, income, education, government, health care and environment. Air quality in the Twin Cities is unsurpassed by that of any like-sized metropolitan area in the United States, and single-family homes in traditional neighborhoods still are the norm. Lacking old-style political machines, politics is clean, if sometimes fiercely competitive, and the populace is well educated, amiable and resourceful.

Many of the same amenities that appeal to residents also draw tourists. The Minnesota Zoo on 500 acres in Apple Valley, with 650 animals from all parts of the world and an overhead monorail, is the state's number-one attraction. Having outgrown several previous homes, the new Science Museum of Minnesota in downtown St. Paul has emerged a world-class science and technology center *cum* natural history museum. Its domed Omnitheater is equipped with the largest and most sophisticated film projection system in the world.

Add major league sports (baseball, football, hockey and soccer), to say nothing of thoroughbred racing at Canterbury Downs, and the Twin Cities probably have something for everyone.

Keeping the skeletons where they properly belong, St. Paul rarely mentions its infamous beginnings. In 1839 downtown St. Paul's first settlers were two Irishmen, one of them a blackguard. Edward Phelan and John Hays were former soldiers at Fort Snelling who took up adjoining claims on the Mississippi, below the present Kellogg Boulevard in St. Paul and extending from Minnesota Street to Eagle Street. Edward Phelan, described as a giant of a man, well above six feet tall, "immoral, cruel, revengeful, and unscrupulous," was the younger of the two, still in his twenties. John Hays, "an honest, good, courteous, and clever old gentleman," considerably smaller, was 40 years old. During several terms in the army, Hays had managed to put aside a tidy purse of money.

These two were St. Paul's Cain and Abel, if you will. When Hays disappeared in the fall of 1839, and his dead body, its head bashed in, washed ashore near Carver's Cave, Phelan was arrested for murder. Although all the evidence clearly pointed to him, when he was tried in

St. Anthony (later Minneapolis) on the east bank of the Mississippi in 1860. UPTON PHOTO; MINNESOTA HISTORICAL SOCIETY

navigation on the Mississippi, with two river landings, the Upper Landing being at the foot of Chestnut and Eagle streets, St. Paul became the region's first major commercial center.

Ten years later, 10 miles upstream, sawmilling and flour milling commenced at St. Anthony Falls. Soldiers from Fort Snelling had had a sawmill on the west side of the river in the 1820s, and the fort's canny sutler, Franklin Steele, later claimed a site on the east bank and built a dam and sawmill there in 1848. Buying up additional claims, Steele platted the town of St. Anthony in 1849, drawing hundreds of settlers. Across the river, once the region was ceded by the Indians in 1851, the west bank soon was lined with mills of its own, and the city of Minneapolis was incorporated in 1856. For a time, there were three rival settlements—St. Paul, St. Anthony and Minneapolis—until St. Anthony threw in its lot with Minneapolis in 1872.

For several decades, its economy tied to trade and river transportation, St. Paul was the larger city. Once the railroads were in place, however, Minneapolis gained the upper hand. With settlement pressing westward, Minneapolis's power site and its location between St. Paul and the farming frontier made it the better choice for new enterprise. In 1869, 15 sawmills at or near St. Anthony Falls were producing more than 100 million board feet of lumber annually, and flour milling was steadily gaining ground. Less than a dozen years later, there were 25 flour mills at the falls, five of them operated by C.A. Pillsbury and Company and another three by Washburn-Crosby and Company (later General Mills). With large, newly-equipped mills, these two firms represented one-half the city's milling capacity.

St. Paul's 19th-century prosperity and character can be laid chiefly to two men, empire builder James J. Hill and Archbishop John Ireland. Working hand in glove with the archbishop to people the Minnesota frontier, Jim Hill made the Twin Cities the hub of an inland railroading network. Railroads also facilitated Minnesota's milling, meat packing and mining industries. Personally, Hill counted enormous personal profits, but he was large-hearted in dispersing them. St. Paul's James J. Hill Reference Library is witness to his generosity, and his gifts to the St. Paul archdiocese included a new Catholic seminary. In the 1980s, his philanthrophy continues through the Northwest Area Foundation, which each year sup-

Prairie du Chien (the seat of Crawford County in Wisconsin Territory, which then extended west to the Mississippi River), he was somehow acquitted of the crime. Subsequently, Phelan moved to a new claim on the St. Paul creek now named for him. His name (only the spelling has been changed) is attached to one of the city's most beautiful lakes, Lake Phalen. In the minds of his neighbors and pioneer St. Paul historian J. Fletcher Williams, there never was any question that Phelan was guilty of St. Paul's first murder.

St. Paul was called Pig's Eye at first, named for a licentious, one-eyed whiskey seller who set up shop at the site of the Lower Landing at Jackson Street. It was only after missionary priest Father Lucian Galtier dedicated the settlement's first rude log chapel to St. Paul, "the apostle of nations," on November 1, 1841, that Pig's Eye, like Saul, became St. Paul. Located at the practical head of

ports area arts and social programs to the tune of several million dollars.

Claiming top billing at the head of Summit Avenue, James J. Hill's gargantuan red stone residence is maintained by the Minnesota Historical Society, which conducts tours of the house. Built at a cost of $280,000 in 1887, it contains 32 rooms, 35 fireplaces, 18 bathrooms, a ballroom and a two-story art gallery with a skylight roof. To the north, having purchased the former Amherst H. Wilder mansion, Archbishop Ireland was Hill's next-door neighbor. From his porch in his declining years, the archbishop watched his new cathedral, designed by French architect Emmanuel Masqueray and begun in 1906, going up across the street. Patterned after St. Peter's in Rome, St. Paul's Cathedral memorializes the accomplishments of Minnesota's greatest churchman.

Born near Kilkenny, Ireland, in 1838, John Ireland was a dominant figure in the religious, social and political life of the United States for more than half a century. He immigrated to this country with his family following the 1840s potato famines, and he was educated in St. Paul by the city's first bishop, Joseph Cretin, who sent the young man to France to study for the priesthood. After distinguishing himself under fire while serving as a chaplain during the Civil War, Father Ireland returned to St. Paul, where he became a leader in the temperance movement and organized a mammoth colonization program that enabled thousands of Irish immigrants to take up farmsteads in southwestern Minnesota.

John Ireland had the ears of several presidents including Harrison, McKinley, Roosevelt and Taft; he lobbied for better wages for workers, religious instruction in the public schools and an end to racial prejudice. He helped ease the takeover of the Catholic Philippine Islands by the United States at the end of the Spanish-American War. In St. Paul, he founded the College of St. Thomas and installed St. Paul's first electric streetcar system to provide transportation to the school, then several miles out in the country.

The second dome embroidering St. Paul's skyline belongs to the Minnesota State Capitol, a classic white marble structure on Wabasha Hill. Completed in 1905, it was designed by Cass Gilbert, who is best-remembered as the architect responsible for the Woolworth Building in New York (which popularized the skyscraper). Before establishing himself in the East, Gilbert got his start in Min-

nesota, designing countless residences, churches and commercial buildings between 1883 and 1910.

The Capitol, with its central dome and rotunda flanked by symmetrical wings, was Gilbert's grandest gift to St. Paul. He insisted on a hefty art budget, and commissioned murals and sculptures by leading artists including Howard Pyle and John Daniels. Outside, Minnesota's best-known sculpture, the four gilded horses (quadriga) at the base of the dome, are the work of Daniel Chester French, the sculptor who created the Lincoln Memorial.

Minnesota politics has had far-ranging consequences, and the state has produced more than its fair share of national leaders. There are two plausible reasons for this. First of all, Minnesota has a longstanding tradition of protest politics, dating to decades of agrarian discon-

Left: Father John Ireland, 1862. LARSON PHOTO; MINNESOTA HISTORICAL SOCIETY

Above: *Looking down John Ireland Boulevard to St. Paul's Cathedral from the roof of the Capitol, inhabited by the golden quadriga. Crowds in front of the capitol are sampling ethnic foods from throughout the state at the Taste of Minnesota festival.* R. HAMILTON SMITH

Iron fence scrollwork frames Conservatory gardens at Como Park in St. Paul.

Jogger circling Lake Calhoun in Minneapolis. R. HAMILTON SMITH PHOTOS

tent during the late 1800s. Secondly, the state's Scandinavian population, its most politically active ethnic group, has historically put its faith in politics and government to solve social problems. (You don't have to be Scandinavian to run for governor in Minnesota, but it certainly helps.)

Since territorial days, when Governor Alexander Ramsey upheld Whig ideals, Minnesotans have embraced a wide range of political faiths, both liberal and conservative. In the late 1860s, responding to the grievances of farmers who felt themselves victimized by the railroads, money lenders and dishonest elevator operators and millers, Oliver H. Kelley of Elk River organized the National Grange. Kelley intended an apolitical association of farmers engaged in cooperative buying and selling, but the Grange spawned several successive political groups, all of them aimed at regulating big business. During the 20th century, large numbers of Minnesota voters have been attracted to three major reform movements: Populism, Progressivism and New Dealism.

Minnesota's Democratic-Farmer-Labor Party (DFL) is something else again. The idea of a third party to represent both farmers and organized labor was talked up in Minnesota as early as the 1880s, finally culminating in the formation of the Farmer-Labor Party following World War I. Farmer-Labor candidates won both U.S. Senate seats in the regular election of 1922 and the special election of 1923 upon the death of incumbent Knute Nelson, but the party's meteoric rise was equalled only by its subsequent decline. Eventually, neither the Farmer-Laborites nor the Democrats posed any real challenge to Minnesota's dominant Republican Party. Deciding to combine their clout, the Farmer-Labor and Democrat parties merged in 1944, re-establishing the pattern of two-party politics in the state.

National newscasters have been known to explain the DFL as what Minnesota calls Democrats, but there's more to it than that. The party's Democrat origins are apparent, but its distinctiveness derives from its Farmer-Labor roots, nurtured by long years of protest politics. As a regional philosophy, it embodies a unique amalgam of Minnesota experience and tradition, and the important thing is that it works. Consider recent presidential contenders Hubert Horatio Humphrey, Eugene McCarthy and Walter Mondale. All three of them came up through DFL ranks in Minnesota.

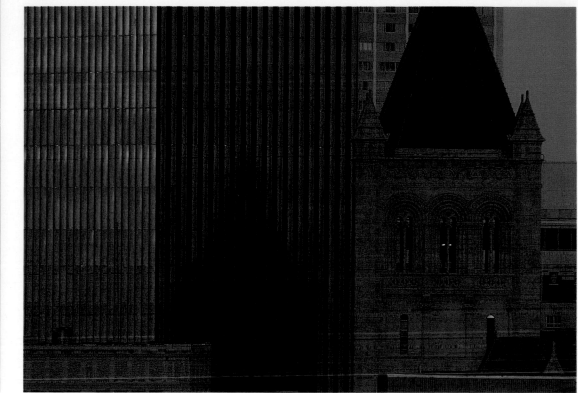

In 1851 when the territorial legislature awarded St. Paul the state capital, Minneapolis (St. Anthony then) got the University of Minnesota. Thinking grandiosely, the early regents commenced building at a rate that brought the school close to bankruptcy. That it survived at all is partly due to John Sargent Pillsbury, university regent, state senator and governor, known today as the "father of the university."

John Sargent was the first of the Pillsburys to settle in Minnesota. Originally from New Hampshire, he opened a hardware store on St. Anthony's Main Street in 1855, but it soon burned to the ground, leaving him $35,000 in debt. Eight years later, having worked his way out of ruin, he held a note for $1,000 due him by contractors for locks, nails and sundry hardware for Old Main. Of a mind to sue the university, he instead agreed to become a regent and helped put the school back onto its feet. In 1869, Pillsbury persuaded his nephew, Charles A. Pills-

bury, to join him in Minnesota, and it was young Charlie who founded Charles A. Pillsbury and Company the next year. John Sargent and Charlie's father, George A. Pillsbury, were partners in the enterprise.

With five campuses (Minneapolis/St. Paul, Duluth, Morris, Crookston and Waseca) and 75,000 undergraduate and graduate students, the university is one of the largest schools in country. Offering degree programs in more than 250 fields, it ranks seventh among public institutions in the United States (according to the National Academy of Sciences), with top programs in such diverse areas as chemical engineering, journalism, geography and architecture. It also is a major research facility. Open-heart surgery was pioneered by doctors at the University of Minnesota Hospitals and School of Medicine. (South African surgeon Christiaan Barnard trained at University Hospitals.) As the world's leading kidney transplant center, it draws patients from around the globe.

Above: St. Paul cityscape with Landmark Center tower in foreground.
Left: *Horse-drawn carriage at Rice Park in downtown St. Paul.*
R. HAMILTON SMITH PHOTOS

masters including Rembrandt, Turner, Constable and Corot, he added room after room to his home until there were 15 galleries and he had to hire a curator. Right on the trolley line, convenient to visitors, Walker's house took up half the block at Eighth Street and Hennepin in what is now the heart of downtown Minneapolis.

When the Minneapolis Institute plans were being drawn, Walker was anxious to donate his entire collection to the new museum. But what happened was that Institute experts proved too picky. Not all of his pieces met their criteria, they said, and that was enough for Walker. If the Institute wouldn't accept his entire collection, it wouldn't get any of it, he promised. In 1927 he built the Walker Art Center, which has become one of the country's leading museums, on Lowry Hill overlooking Loring Park. Reflecting changing times, later generations of Walkers have steered the museum's focus to contemporary art—with spectacular success. In 1980 the Walker Art Center originated the Picasso exhibition that later traveled to the Museum of Modern Art in New York.

When it comes to funding the arts, Twin City businesses happily pick up part of the tab. In 1976 the Greater Minneapolis Chamber of Commerce created the Five Percent Club to recognize Minnesota firms that donate five percent of their taxable incomes to community causes. The first program of its kind in the country, the Five Percent Club since has been copied coast to coast. In Minnesota, the giving actually had been going on quietly for some years. The Dayton-Hudson Corporation, for instance, has been returning five percent of its pretax earnings to the community since 1946. Companies contribute to a wide variety of recipients, but an annual total of about $20 million has been earmarked for the arts in recent years.

A recent tally counts some 50 theaters, 160 galleries and 30 dance companies in the Twin Cities, and the towns also support two brilliant orchestras. Dividing their talents between the twins, the Minnesota Orchestra led by Edo de Waart plays at Orchestra Hall on Nicollet Mall in Minneapolis, while the St. Paul Chamber Orchestra takes its bows across the river at the Ordway Music Theatre. A 1980s addition to St. Paul, fronting Rice Park, the Ordway has been described as "a glittering jewel of glass, copper and mahogany." Both Orchestra Hall and the Ordway also book leading classical, jazz and pop musicians.

Above: *The American Swedish Institute in Minneapolis was the private residence of Swan Turnbladh, an immigrant from Sweden who made his fortune as the owner of a local Swedish-language newspaper.*
Facing page, top: *Peavey Plaza at Orchestra Hall in Minneapolis*
Bottom left: *The Investors Diversified Tower viewed through a window of the Minneapolis Institute of Arts.*
Bottom right: *Trompe l'oeil 19th-century facades painted on side of downtown St. Paul Building.*
R. HAMILTON SMITH PHOTOS

Governor John Sargent Pillsbury's nephew, Alfred F. Pillsbury, was the family's first art connoisseur, helping put the state on a proper cultural footing. He served on the board of Charles A. Pillsbury and Company, but his collection of Chinese bronzes and the Minneapolis Institute of Arts, to which he left it, took precedence. Dating from the early 1880s, the Institute is the center of Minnesota's thriving cultural network. A classic monumental public building in the Beaux Arts tradition, it houses a collection of 65,000 objects representing nearly all schools and periods of art including European and American paintings, sculpture, decorative arts and period rooms.

Minneapolis's second major art gallery is the result of a public-relations blunder. In 1879 lumberman Thomas Barlow Walker opened a room in his home to anyone who wanted to see his art collection. In the years to come, buying up dozens upon dozens of paintings by

When Sir Tyrone Guthrie was searching for his promised land in the late 1950s, he found it in the Twin Cities. Broadway bored him, he said, and he was looking for fertile ground for a repertory theater. John J. Cowles, who had just succeeded his father as editor of the Minneapolis *Star and Tribune,* was among those persons wanting to lure Guthrie to Minneapolis, and he took the project to the children and grandchildren of T.B. Walker. When Cowles asked them for land adjacent to the Walker Art Center and $400,000 toward a new theater, they agreed on the condition that he raise additional monies in the community. Even schoolchildren sent in their donations. Now in its third decade, the Guthrie Theater is among the most celebrated professional theaters in the country. Resident actors present a rotating repertory of plays, and it often is possible to see as many as three plays in a weekend.

More than a few Twin Cities people have made names for themselves in the entertainment industry. Comedian Louie Anderson is a hometown boy made good, and curvaceous Loni Anderson is a former Miss Roseville (of the St. Paul suburb). Lew Ayres, Ann Sothern, Arlene Dahl, the Arness brothers (James Arness and Peter Graves), and the singing Andrews Sisters all got their starts in the Twin Cities. Both Eddie Heimberger and Avrom Hirsch Goldbogen sold newspapers in Minneapolis. They became better known as Eddie Albert and Mike Todd. Robert Vaughn is from Minneapolis, and Linda Kelsey, Billie Newman of *Lou Grant,* is from St. Paul.

Architecturally, the Twin Cities parade the past and present moods of an ever-changing urban environment with aplomb. Minnesota's first houses, most of them frame structures, copied Federal or Greek Revival patterns, though German immigrants preferred simple brick or stone structures. The heavily bracketed Italianate style came next, utilized for public and commercial buildings as well as residences. (Through the 1890s, Italianate was considered the only style for county courthouses and government buildings.) In the 1870s Minnesotans were exploring French Second Empire themes, the Alexander Ramsey House in Irvine Park in St. Paul being the finest house of its kind in the state. But this was before Richardsonian Romanesque patterns became the rage.

By the mid-1890s architect Harvey Ellis and others were transforming downtown Minneapolis and St. Paul

into stately Romanesque Revival areas. More avant-garde when it came to residential dwellings, these same architects mastered the fanciful Queen Anne style, the epitome of the picturesque. In the decades that followed, Minnesotans embraced additional styles that reminded them of their collective heritage: Tudor, Georgian, Colonial and Beaux Arts. But a funny thing happened on the way to the 1930s. The American Skyscraper style with Art Deco detailing became the favorite for important Twin Cities office buildings. St. Paul's nationally acclaimed Ramsey County Courthouse and City Hall is a superb example. Actually, Minnesota (and American) architecture had reached a turning point. Taking leave of traditional formats, it confidently shook off Old World influences to begin shaping an indigenous architecture of the future.

But by the 1950s, both Minneapolis and St. Paul needed to revitalize their aging core areas. Families who could afford to do so were moving to the suburbs, while some people who stayed were living in overcrowded, substandard housing. The Washington Avenue skid row in Minneapolis, home to 3,000 people, was one of the largest in the country, and the neighborhood surrounding the capitol in St. Paul was crowded with tenements. Unfortunately, a number of architectural landmarks—including the famed Metropolitan Building in Minneapolis and the old Ryan Hotel in St. Paul—were lost in the renewal process, but recycling has resulted in a virtual rebirth of the Twin Cities downtown areas.

In Minneapolis, Gateway Center, the nation's most ambitious downtown redevelopment project when it began, replaced skid row, and for the first time in 50 years new housing (albeit it apartments and condominiums) went up in the central city. Nicollet Avenue, the busiest retail street in the Upper Midwest, became a tree-lined mall for pedestrians and buses, and a second-story climate-controlled skyway system connected most downtown buildings, making winter considerably easier for both residents and visitors.

St. Paul's renewal programs began in the late 1940s when the city started razing its slums. St. Paul, too, relies on an enclosed downtown skyway system, and its Capital Centre Renewal Project, encompassing a twelve-block downtown area, has attracted substantial new development. Opening in 1987, the 37-story World Trade Center enhances the city's progressive image.

Little thought had been given to preserving historic structures when renewal projects began in the 1950s, but the loss and threatened loss of several major buildings prompted concern on both sides of the Mississippi. Minneapolis lost the ornate Metropolitan Building, the tallest structure west of Chicago when it was completed in 1890, as well as its turn-of-the-century Romanesque Revival downtown library, but the public outcry that followed resulted in a second chance for other historic structures. The old Butler Brothers warehouse, now Butler Square, was converted to office and retail space, and a warehouse complex on the riverfront became St. Anthony Main, a festive collage of shops and eateries. In St. Paul, the old Federal Courts Building on Rice Park was saved from the wreckers' ball and rehabilitated as Landmark Center (for the arts), while the city's great gray-stone railroad depot, dressed with Doric columns, now leases space to several fine restaurants.

Whole neighborhoods got on the preservation bandwagon. F. Scott Fitzgerald once described St. Paul's Summit Avenue as "a museum of American architectural failures," but its residents don't see it that way. One of this country's truly great streets, it is likely the best-preserved Victorian boulevard in America. Fitzgerald lived in a red stone rowhouse at 599 Summit (which now bears a plaque to his memory) while writing his first novel, *This Side of Paradise,* but his feelings for the street were ambivalent at best. Preoccupied as he was in his stories with the lives of the rich, he had grown up on the fringes of St. Paul society and always felt himself an outsider. Today, given the gigantic dimensions of many Summit Avenue houses, some of them have been converted to condominiums.

In the late 1970s, restaurateur Bill Naegele started a renaissance of his own by opening Forepaugh's, one of St. Paul's most popular restaurants, in the former Joseph Forepaugh mansion in Irvine Park. Built in 1870, the three-story Victorian residence had badly deteriorated, as had the entire neighborhood. Before Naegele purchased and gutted the house, it had been divided into light-housekeeping apartments. In its heyday in the 1870s, Irvine Park was St. Paul's most exclusive address, and Joseph Forepaugh a wealthy wholesale merchant. His closest neighbor was Alexander Ramsey, Minnesota's first territorial governor, who built the massive gray-stone French Second Empire house across the street.

By the mid-1970s, except for the Ramsey House, now a Minnesota Historical Society site, Irvine Park was a shambles. Fire had claimed a number of the homes, and many of the others stood empty on overgrown lots. The city had thoughts of razing the remaining structures and starting over, but that didn't happen. Instead, the block-sized park that is central to this community has been refurbished, its stately iron fountain and gazebo replaced, and the historic houses surrounding it have been lovingly rehabilitated. Not all of the present houses in Irvine Park are the original ones. In some cases, historic houses from nearby neighborhoods have been moved to Irvine Park, bringing a rich architectural diversity to the neighborhood.

The Minnesota Twins play baseball indoors these days, at the Hubert H. Humphrey Metrodome in downtown Minneapolis.

Facing page: *Downtown Minneapolis on the west bank of the Mississippi River, with the 57-story Investors Diversified Tower in the background.*
R. HAMILTON SMITH PHOTOS

A country church near Lanesboro.
CHARLES J. JOHNSTON

Fog filling the valleys of southeastern Minnesota. R. HAMILTON SMITH

Facing page: *The farming community of New Prague was settled by immigrants from Czechoslovakia.*
R. HAMILTON SMITH

grants upriver from Galena, Illinois, to Minnesota ports, it was the point of arrival for many pioneers. Stately 19th-century homes attest to its early success as a grain and lumber center. (You can tour the Watkins mansion, completed in the 1920s by the family famous worldwide for medicines, spices and personal-care products.) Currently, Winona's population is about 25,000; small manufacturing firms, two Catholic colleges and Winona State University (the oldest college west of the Mississippi, dating from 1860) provide the town's economic underpinnings.

Once or twice a year, my husband Charlie and I drive to Winona just to eat at the Hot Fish Shop. Winona has a strong Polish community, and on Christmas night, 1931, Henry Kowalewski and his wife Helen, gambling what little money they had, opened their first Hot Fish Shop on the present site of the Washington-Kosciusko grade school. Located at the intersection of highways 14-61 and 43 in the shadow of Winona's Sugar Loaf Mountain, the present restaurant remains in the family and still uses the Kowalewskis' original recipes for batter-fried fish and tartar sauce. Customers arrive in helicopters and limousines, and you see numerous out-of-state license plates in the parking lot. But don't expect fancy. This is your ordinary everyday restaurant with some Polish trimmings added. What you will get is superb, first-rate batter-fried fish.

It is obvious from its craggy topography that most of southeastern Minnesota was not covered by the last glacial advance. Possibly, this "driftless area," including the area south and east of Winona—also parts of Wisconsin, Iowa and Illinois—was bypassed by glacial activity altogether. Geologists theorize that uplands to the northwest and northeast deflected the south-flowing ice. As its name implies, this region has virtually no glacial drift—no moraines, till plains, round boulders or sandy outwash plains. Paleozoic bedrock is close to the surface in the driftless area, and preglacial steam valleys, buried elsewhere, were only enlarged by glacial meltwaters.

Southeastern Minnesota also is characterized by irregular pock-marked karst topography. Fillmore County alone has an estimated 5,750 sinkholes, many of them dotting corn and alfalfa fields. Less mysterious than it seems, karst is the result of dissolved limestone, developing in regions with moderate to heavy rainfall where limestone formations occur at or near the surface. Falling rain takes in atmospheric carbon, becoming slightly

Above: The Root River Valley. The Root's south branch is one of Minnsota's premier trout streams.
R. HAMILTON SMITH

Right: Mrs. B's Bed and Breakfast in historic Lanesboro on the Root River.
CHARLES J. JOHNSTON

Owing to its ancient topography, the southeastern triangle contains some of Minnesota's best trout streams. South and west of Winona, Forestville State Park in Fillmore County, is a place better than most to cast a line. Encompassing several hundred acres of mature hardwood forests bordering three clean, spring-fed trout streams (Canfield Creek, Forestville Creek and the South Branch Root River), the park takes its name from the ghost town of Forestville within its boundaries.

Forestville hit its peak in the late 1850s when it had two stores, two hotels, two sawmills, a grist mill, and even a distillery and a tavern. But it was all downhill from there. When the railroad bypassed Forestville, and it lost its bid for county seat, its doom was sealed. Its main attraction is Tom Meighen's mercantile store—now maintained by the Minnesota Historical Society—which closed for business on a May evening in 1910. Still on its shelves is a wealth of 19th-century paraphernalia—sidesaddles, ox yokes, a spinning wheel, a Civil War drum and a horse's straw hat.

Whenever my husband Charlie and I are in this part of southeastern Minnesota (and this is frequently because Charlie's real passion is trout fishing), our second home is Mrs. B.'s, a Bed and Breakfast in Lanesboro. Proving that you can indeed make a silk purse from a sow's ear, Mrs. B's is an 1870s limestone building, a furniture store and mortuary that owners Jack and Nancy Bratrud remodeled to accommodate nine guest rooms, each with private bath. Furnished with four-poster beds, rolltop desks and all the trimmings, the bedrooms are the kind you see pictured in country-home magazines.

Less than two hours from the Twin Cities, and a half hour from Rochester, Lanesboro is off to a recent start as a tourist town, but the town's definitely a comer. Nestled in a bowl-shaped valley in a crook of the Root River, complete with steepled churches on a high hill overlooking prim, white-painted Victorian frame houses, it looks to be a Grant Wood painting incarnate. Next door to Mrs. B's on Parkway North, David Leach operates Just Plain Folk, a gallery specializing in Amish furniture, quilts and the faceless Amish dolls. Living on farms near Lanesboro, the Amish add a colorful new dimension to Lanesboro's appeal. But they hardly are part of the town's past.

Lanesboro's first settler was an Irishman named John Scanlon, who built himself a log cabin with a thatched

acidic, and this acidity increases as the water seeps into the ground, picking up carbon dioxide from soil, air and decomposing vegetation. Once limestone comes in contact with this slightly acidic water, it rapidly disintegrates, resulting in sinkholes, caves and labyrinths of underground tunnels and channels.

From a distance, sinkholes appear to be sinking, circular patches of trees. Up close, they are steep, rocky funnels, 30′ to 150′ in diameter. Heavy rainfalls turn these sinkholes into dark, swirling eddies that dissipate underground. Minnesota also has more than 300 known caves, three of them commercial ventures open to the public. In Fillmore County, Mystery Cave, which has more than 15 miles of mapped passageways, and Niagara Cave, with a large underground waterfall, both are limestone caves. A third commercial cave is in Stillwater; formed in sandstone, it was once used for aging beer.

RED WING

It would be hard to find a prettier river town than Red Wing. Minnesota's globe-trotting geographer Cotton Mather calls it "one of the most appealing, enticing, comfortable, and delightful spots in America." Named for a dynasty of Indian chiefs whose village previously inhabited this choice Mississippi River site, Red Wing is small-town U.S.A. at its best. At the present time, this city of 13,000 residents is in the midst of an energetic revival to restore its Victorian image.

In the 1830s the last chief Red Wing, convinced that civilization would benefit his people, welcomed white missionary families to his valley. Short years later, treaties signed with the Minnesota Dakota in 1851 left his band homeless, consigned to a reservation along the upper Minnesota River. Pioneer farming families flocked to the area, and pretty Red Wing came of age as a farm trade center. By the early 1870s the town was reportedly the largest primary wheat market in the world. Mining the nearby gray clay deposits,

Red Wing also became famous as a pottery maker, producing sturdy crocks, pots and jars. A union-led workers' strike led to the shutdown of the last pottery in 1967, but this has only inflated the price of Red Wing pottery, cherished by collectors nationwide.

Once the railroads reached the prairies, Red Wing declined as a wheat market, but by then the city had attracted various firms including a tannery (still in business), an iron works, a wagon and carriage shop, a sorghum mill, a brewery and a pork-packing plant. For the past several decades the Red Wing Shoe Company, a locally-owned company founded in 1905, famous for its work shoes and boots and Irish Setter sports boots, has been the city's largest employer. The shoe company is also Red Wing's leading benefactor, responsible for the multi-million dollar renovation of the historic St. James Hotel on Main Street.

As expected, the refurbished St. James proved the keystone in the city's current

preservation program. The city has designated three historic districts, with private citizens undertaking numerous commercial restoration projects. Residents in older neighborhoods are putting time and money into rehabilitating their homes. On Highway 61, a Hardee's hamburger restaurant does business in the former Chicago Great Western

Depot. Downtown, a recently-acquired turn-of-the-century California cable car operates on Main Street. Catering to sightseers, one of the last wooden riverboats, the *Pretty Red Wing,* plies the city's harbor.

As Red Wing sees it, the surest bet for the future lies in remembering and building on its colorful past.

The Mississippi River at Red Wing.
CHARLES J. JOHNSTON

58

roof and dirt floor here in 1856. A dozen years later investors with an eye to ready profits formed a townsite company in New York, and the town took shape in zip time, a three-story stone hotel going up in a wheat field before harvest time. The railroad came to town that same year, and city fathers put a stone dam on the Root River, erecting two large flour mills that ran day and night. By 1879 Lanesboro had five hotels and 1,600 residents. At the present time, the Lanesboro Fish Hatchery occupies one of the old mill sites (it supplies nearly all of the trout stocked in Minnesota streams), and Lanesboro's population hovers around 1,000.

Buffalo Bill Cody is said to have staged a wild west show in Lanesboro in 1877, six years before he organized "Buffalo Bill's Wild West." Cody was in town to visit an old friend, Dr. David F. Powell, a local physician who dressed in fringed buckskins and advertised that he could straighten crossed eyes "in one minute." Powell was on friendly terms with local Winnebagos camped east of town, having been initiated into their tribe; the Indians called him "White Beaver." Standing atop Lanesboro's north bluff and looking down upon the town's natural amphitheater one fine spring day, Cody and Powell decided to present a wild west show. Powell supplied the Indians, Cody trained them, and this first exhibition played in the streets of Lanesboro.

A second southeastern Minnesota river town has a wild-west story of its own. West of Red Wing on the Cannon River, Northfield is the town that foiled the Jesse James gang. On September 7, 1876, eight gunmen including Jesse, his brother Frank and the three Younger brothers, galloped into town prepared to rob the First National Bank. Cashier Joseph Lee Heywood proved the hero of the piece, refusing to unlock the safe, for which he was shot dead. The bandits also wounded bank teller Alonzo E. Bunker, but by then local merchants had hastily armed themselves with rifles, shotguns and rocks. A streetfight ensued, leaving two of the robbers dead and two others wounded.

Within seven minutes of their arrival, the remaining gunmen were riding out of town (without any loot), pursued at high speed by a posse (which a few days later numbered 1,000 men). Jesse and Frank made their getaway, but the remaining gang members were rounded up two weeks later at Hanska Slough in Brown County. Whooping it up the first weekend after Labor Day each

fall, Northfield draws thousands of visitors for its "Defeat of Jesse James Days."

Nationally, Northfield is better-known for its two top-ranking private colleges, Carleton and St. Olaf. Originally affiliated with the Congregational Church, Carleton College opened in 1866. Norwegian Lutheran immigrants founded St. Olaf in 1874. Famous contemporaries on the faculty at St. Olaf, F. Melius Christiansen and O.E. Rölvaag both achieved worldwide acclaim, Christiansen for his music, Rölvaag for his fiction (especially *Giants in the Earth*).

With a current population of about 13,000, swelled by 4,500 each school year, Northfield dates to 1855. It was founded by eastern entrepreneur John North who saw its potential as a flour-milling center. In more recent years, the Malt-o-Meal company has taken the place of the riverside flour mills, supplying breakfast cereal to an international market. With many fine dairy farms in the area, Northfield was known as the "Holstein Center of America" in the early 1900s. Playing down the cows, today's community prides itself on its culture and common sense.

Threshing rig and crew near Plainview, September 1898.
MINNESOTA HISTORICAL SOCIETY

Facing page, left: The Whitewater River Valley near the town of Ellen.
R. HAMILTON SMITH
Top: Wild turkeys were successfully reintroduced into southeastern Minnesota in the 1960s. DANIEL J. COX
Bottom: Winter is comfortable for thousands of Canada geese on Silver Lake in Rochester, portions of which are kept ice-free by warm water from the city's power plant. DANIEL & JULIE COX

MINNESOTA'S AMISH

Usually, the photographs you see of Amish people portray sober, dour-faced people. The reason for this is not that the Amish are all that somber. But the strict rule of Amish life simply forbids photographs. "When we see a camera pointed towards us, we'll either turn away, or at least we'll stop smiling," one man explains.

In the past couple of years, my husband Charlie and I have met several Amish families in southeastern Minnesota. We've picnicked with them, ridden in their buggies, and visited in their homes, but we have yet to get any really good photos detailing Amish life.

It isn't that we haven't tried. One afternoon last winter, we even happened on a near-perfect opportunity. Driving in "Amish country," we saw a young Amish boy with a team of horses pulling a manure spreader across a large field. He rode against a backdrop of billowing clouds in a darkening sky. You couldn't ask for a better picture. He was already out of camera range by the time Charlie stopped the car and grabbed his camera, so we waited while the boy emptied the spreader on the far side of the field. Meantime, Charlie positioned the car so that he could get a close-up shot as the boy came back across the field, heading to the barn. With the boy in his camera sights, Charlie snapped the shutter. Only to realize that he was out of film.

Or picture this. On a recent visit with one family, the talk turned to funeral arrangements for a neighbor man who had died the night before. What with the man's relatives coming from Ohio, this would possibly be the biggest funeral the community had seen, the husband said—75 or 80 buggies. Amish people are buried from their own homes, he told us, and the oak coffins never are made ahead of time. The same man appointed by the bishop to make the coffins (wide at the shoulders and narrow at the feet, with a hinged top lid that folds down for viewing) also maintains the carriage that bears the coffin to the cemetery.

The weather was dismal the day of the funeral, with patches of snow lingering in the fields. But Charlie and I, staying home where we belonged, can only imagine that picturesque procession. It embarrasses me that we would want to intrude on Amish privacy to the point of photographing a funeral. But the historian in me keeps wishing Charlie and his camera were sometimes invisible.

The first half-dozen Amish families who settled in south-eastern Minnesota came from Ohio in the mid-1970s. Overcrowded where they were, and unable to afford rising Ohio land prices, they were looking for well watered, rolling farmland, similar to the country they were leaving. Since then their Minnesota settlement has grown to nearly 80 families, from New York, Michigan and Ontario. The community runs diagonally from just north of Mabel near the Iowa border northwest almost to Preston in Fillmore County. This is Minnesota's only Amish settlement, and local merchants have discovered they have a tourist attraction in their midst. One company offers tours of Amish homes.

The Amish live simply, doing things much the way they have for centuries. When an Amish family buys a farm, the electricity comes out. They don't use radios, televisions or telephones. The women dress in long, dark dresses fastened with straight pins, not buttons, and cover their hair with white caps. Amish men and boys wear black trousers held up by suspenders, and broad-brimmed hats—straw in summer and black felt for winter. Unmarried men are clean-shaven; married men wear beards but not moustaches.

Most Amish men in Fillmore County operate dairy

farms, using horses instead of tractors. Their wives tend children and gardens, canning produce and sewing for their families on treadle machines. A few of the men are master furniture makers, turning out finely-crafted Amish furniture in small home workshops. Some of the women make hand-stitched pieced quilts for sale. Traditionally, Amish quilters prefer bold geometric designs, using dark, solid colors (one of my favorites is the Virginia Star). Some of these quilts are sold in local shops and in Rochester; others are sent to Amish stores in Pennsylvania.

At home, unless they have English-speaking visitors, the Amish speak a Pennsylvania-Dutch dialect of German. This is the only language the children know until they go to school. Once they reach school age, Amish children learn to read and write both English and German in one-room Amish schools, which they attend through the eighth grade. This is the extent of their formal education. Because children either walk to school or their parents bring them by buggy, there are six small schools in the Minnesota community. The Amish do not use school buses.

Incidentally, most of the fit-looking horses you see pulling Amish buggies are former race horses. Typical riding horses are too slow on the road, one Amish man points out. "They either want to gallop or trot real slow. Sometimes we like to go a little faster. This is what we use instead of a car, and we have to get from place to place eventually."

Above: *A buggy in downtown Lanesboro is quiet proof that Minnesota's sole Amish settlement is in this area.*

Facing page: *Amish buggy keeping to the shoulder in fog.* CHARLES J. JOHNSTON PHOTOS

A September scene in St. Croix River State Park. TOM TILL

61

SOUTHWESTERN MINNESOTA
SPEAKING OF FARMING

You'll know right away this is farm country. Bordered by the Minnesota River to the north, these 16 counties boast some of the richest black soils and most productive farms in the world. Glacial drift up to 100′ thick overlies most of southwestern Minnesota, and the soil has been richening these past thousands of years, assimilating decayed plant and animal matter. Average rainfall is 24″ along the western border and 28″ in south-central Minnesota. The growing season varies from 140 to 150 days.

A rolling-plains region with checkerboard fields surrounding tree-enclosed farmsteads, this is the heart of Minnesota's Corn Belt. Planting their fields to corn, soybeans, oats and hay, farmers raise hogs, beef and dairy cattle, and also poultry. Fields of peas and sweet corn carpet south-central Minnesota, and flax is grown in the western counties. The canning industry also is booming. Minnesota grows more sweet corn for processing than any other state and is second only to Wisconsin in green pea production. At Blue Earth, near the Iowa border in Faribault County, a 55 $^{1}/_{2}$'-high statue of the Jolly Green Giant plugs the town's largest employer, the Pillsbury Green Giant Company, which has been canning corn and peas in several southern Minnesota communities for more than 50 years.

Before white settlement, lush virgin prairie dotted with islands of marsh stretched from horizon to horizon. Bison, elk and deer grazed the grasslands, while the wetlands harbored muskrat, mink, beaver and otter. Huge populations of ducks and geese nested in the marshes and creek bottoms, and shorebirds and songbirds brightened the landscape. To the east, the tall grasses could hide a man on horseback. Farther west, in short-grass country, prairie grasses grew two to three feet high. Undisturbed for eons, tangled root systems tested early plows. Pioneer farming families built their first homes and barns with tough prairie sod. Wheat was the staple pioneer crop. (By the late 1870s, 70 percent of Minnesota cropland was in wheat.)

"Wet prairies" were an intricate part of the prairie landscape. As it retreated northward, the last glacier spread low moraines—irregular accumulations of glacial drift—across much of southwestern Minnesota. Spring rains and melting snow filled the hollows between these moraines with water, resulting in myriad small lakes, sloughs and poorly drained bottomland that remained marshy into summer. Wet prairies too damp to plant in spring were used as summer pasturage for dairy cows. Once it became more profitable to raise livestock than wheat, however, farmers began draining the wetlands. The idea was to raise more grain to feed more cattle and hogs. More than 20 percent of the agricultural land in 16 southern Minnesota counties now is underlain with long, branching lines of hollow tile. Except for a few isolated wetlands being preserved as wildlife habitat by state and federal agencies, the prairies have been drained.

Minnesota farm statistics are impressive. Minnesota is among the top six states in beef cattle, hog, grain corn and soybean production. Ranking seventh nationwide, Minnesota annually exports agricultural products worth more than $1.6 billion, primarily feed grains, soybeans and soybean products, and wheat and wheat products. In

Twilight harvesting. R. HAMILTON SMITH

1986 corn yields of 122 bushels per acre broke the previous year's record, and Minnesota turkey growers raised a record 34.2 million birds. The typical Minnesota farm is 323 acres (somewhat smaller than the national average since many are livestock- or dairy-oriented), and is worth about $250,000.

Rosy statistics cannot hide the fact that many Minnesota farm families currently face economic peril, however. Some very un-rosy figures are actually staggering. For one thing, the number of farms is dropping sharply. Minnesota currently has 93,000 farms, down from 104,000 in 1980. (Wisconsin, Iowa, Illinois and Nebraska likewise have lost many thousands of farms.) In southwestern Minnesota, the price of farmland plummeted from nearly $2,100 per acre in 1981 to something less than $700 in 1986. Average net income per farm is only slightly more than $12,000, and Minnesota's farm debt-to-asset ratio, a whopping 36 percent, is the highest in the nation.

Facing page, left: *Ladybug.*
CONNIE WANNER

Right: R. HAMILTON SMITH

Above: Cropland mosaic with wind breaks. IMAGERY
Right: Abandoned country school-house. CHARLES J. JOHNSTON

Facing page: Rock Valley country church. CONNIE WANNER

Across the country, present farm problems date to the early 1970s when escalating U.S. grain exports sent farmland prices soaring. Both farmers and lenders expected the high level of exports would continue, and many farmers invested heavily in land at rapidly increasing prices. Average Minnesota farmland values shot from $248 per acre in 1972 to a high of $1,310 in 1981. When export demand slackened in the early 1980s, surplus supplies developed, and land prices fell. Farmers were left holding bank notes (some at high interest rates, only compounding their problems) for property worth half what they had paid for it.

In an unprecedented move that will aid thousands of farmers facing foreclosure, Farm Credit Services (FCS) in St. Paul plans to restructure $1 billion in farm loans during 1987 and 1988. Introducing shared-appreciation mortgages, FCS will reduce loan principals to current market values and cut interest rates in exchange for a percentage of the profits if the property increases in value

over a negotiated term of five to 10 years. Assuming $150,000 per loan, more than 6,000 district farmers (in Minnesota, North Dakota, Wisconsin and Michigan) will have their loans restructured under the program.

A state program to restructure farm debt also is being launched. Dealing directly with lenders (including the Federal Land Bank), the State of Minnesota is offering subsidies of up to $50,000 per qualifying loan, to lenders who will write new eight-year loans on debts, using current land values. The portion of the original loan in excess of current land values will be set aside for eight years. If property values do not increase in that time, that portion will be forgiven.

Taking in most or part of six Minnesota counties—also adjacent parts of South Dakota and Iowa—southwest Minnesota's best-known physical feature is a hilly, flatiron-shaped upland that 18th-century explorers called Coteau des Prairies or Highland of the Prairies. Covered by glacial drift as much as 700′ thick, the Coteau reaches a height of 500′ to 800′ above the surrounding till plain, giving rise to numerous small streams that cut deep wooded gorges along its eastern edge. Much of the Coteau also is underlain by uptilted ridges of Sioux quartzite, the remains of an ancient mountain range.

A hard Precambrian sandstone, usually pinkish but varying from almost white to a reddish-purple color, Sioux quartzite is probably about 1.5 billion years old. Geologists believe that it formed in shallow water, possibly on the edge of a shallow sea. Along with other midwestern quartzites, it is significant because it indicates that this portion of North America was relatively quiet and stable during late Precambrian times. Unlike earlier eras, it did not see mountain ranges or lava extrusions being thrust up. Outcroppings of Sioux quartzite can be seen at Pipestone National Monument, the Jeffers Petroglyphs site, and Blue Mounds State Park. (Blue Mounds also maintains one of Minnesota's two state buffalo herds; the other is at Itasca State Park.)

Pierre Charles Le Sueur was the earliest French fur trader and explorer to reach the Minnesota Valley, ascending the Mississippi from the Gulf of Mexico in 1700. Building Fort L'Huillier at the junction of the Minnesota and Blue Earth rivers, near the present city of Mankato, he traded guns, axes, tobacco and pipes to the Dakota for beaver "robes" (nine skins sewed together). Le Sueur also mined what he thought was copper ore, shipping two tons of blue-colored clay to France, only to find that it was utterly worthless. Later, British and as many as a dozen American fur posts did business in the Minnesota Valley. Well known American traders included Philander Prescott, Joseph Renville and Joseph R. Brown.

Until the infamous treaties of Traverse des Sioux and Mendota, southwestern Minnesota remained Indian country. As soon as Minnesota Territory was organized in 1849, farmers, speculators, townsite promoters and fur traders all had begun to clamor for cession of the "Suland." Two years later, pressured by government officials who pointed out that the government had sufficient soldiers to simply take their land, the Dakota signed away 24 million acres, roughly the southern third of Minnesota. In exchange they received a narrow strip of land for two reservations along the Minnesota River and were promised annual payments of goods and money. From the beginning, it was an impossible scheme that ended

The Minnesota River, major feeder of the upper Mississippi.

Farmstead in snowstorm. Winters in southwestern Minnesota may provide as little as 40" of snow, 30" less than in the northeast.
R. HAMILTON SMITH PHOTOS

tragically for the Indians. White settlers took up farmsteads, while the government established the Upper Sioux and Lower Sioux agencies on the reservations to help transform the Indians into self-sufficient farmers. By 1860 both agencies were thriving prairie towns, each populated by nearly 100 white and mixed-blood employees and their families, with more than 7,000 Dakota on the reservations. Some of the Indians lived in government-built houses, but most of them remained in their tipis. Very few of them were really interested in tilling the soil. Much of the little farming being done was accomplished by government employees.

Then in 1858, the year that Minnesota achieved statehood, the reservation area was halved by a new treaty. Indian resentment against the government was growing, and a crop failure in 1861 followed by a winter of near-starvation set the stage for revolt. When summer came, and their expected annuity goods and money were long overdue, the Indians were driven to desperation. "If they are hungry, let them eat grass," remarked storekeeper Andrew J. Myrick at the Lower Sioux Agency. Days later, on August 18, when a band of Indians stormed the Lower Sioux Agency, they shot Myrick dead and stuffed his mouth with grass.

The ensuing Dakota War lasted almost six weeks with major conflicts at Fort Ridgely, New Ulm and Birch Coulee. Raiding the frontier from the Iowa border to Fort Abercrombie on the west bank of the Red River in Dakota Territory, hostile Indians killed hundreds of settlers, looting their homesteads and taking women and children prisoners. After losing a final battle at Wood Lake, many of the Indians fled west or to Canada. Meanwhile, white vengeance was vented on those who remained. Issuing its decisions in quick order, a military commission headed by Henry Sibley sentenced 300 Indians to death. President Lincoln commuted most of these sentences to prison terms, but 38 Dakota were hanged in front of a cheering crowd at Mankato on December 26, 1862.

Those Dakota people remaining in Minnesota, many of whom had come to the aid of whites during the war, were stripped of their reservation land and summarily ousted from the state. Herded aboard overcrowded boats, they were shipped downriver to St. Louis, then up the Missouri to a desolate place called Crow Creek (in what is now southeastern South Dakota), where many of them died. As early as 1869 a few of the Indians began trickling back to their Minnesota homelands. Today there are four small Dakota communities in the state, at Prairie Island near Red Wing, Prior Lake, Morton and Granite Falls.

Fear of further Indian troubles virtually halted immigration in southwestern Minnesota in the years immediately following the Dakota War, but the Homestead Act helped bring a rush of settlers to the area during the late 1870s and 1880s. The railroads laid track westward to the Dakotas, and immigrants from a variety of European countries planted ethnic communities up and down the region. Icelanders settled at Minneota, English at Fairmont, and Belgians at Ghent. German immigrants colonized New Ulm, and Dutchmen founded Edgerton, Worthington and Hollandale. Between 1876 and 1881, Bishop John Ireland, St. Paul's first Catholic archbishop, undertook a mammoth colonization project that brought thousands of Catholic families, most of them Irish, to farms in southwestern Minnesota. Eager to promote Catholic settlement in Minnesota, Archbishop Ireland also hoped to better the lot of Irish immigrants toiling in eastern industrial slums by enabling them to take up farmsteads in the young state. Signing contracts with five Minnesota railroads that named him their exclusive agent for railroad lands in Swift, Big Stone, Lyon, Murray and Nobles counties, the prelate established 10 villages and farming communities: De Graff, Clontarf, Graceville, Minneota, Ghent, Currie, Avoca, Iona, Fulda and Adrian. Peopled today by descendants of early colonists, all of them remain flourishing Catholic centers.

In 1956, Minnesota's first Hutterite farming colony was founded on 1,800 acres near Graceville by several families from Ethan, South Dakota. Known as the Big Stone Farmer Cooperative, the colony consists of 80 people who hold their property in common, speak German and maintain their own schools.

Contemporary dress, radios, magazines and cosmetics are frowned upon, but the Hutterites nonetheless operate their farms using modern farm machinery. Tour groups are welcome any day except Sunday. You will be asked not to photograph colonists, but you likely can obtain permission to take pictures of landscapes that include buildings and machinery. For directions, call the Big Stone Farmer Cooperative: (612) 748-7961.

With nearly 30,000 residents, Mankato (the name derives from the Dakota word meaning blue earth) is

JEFFERS PETROGLYPHS

BOB EIKUM

The Jeffers Petroglyphs in Cottonwood County are Minnesota's largest known concentration of aboriginal rock art. More than 2,000 figures and designs are pecked into an outcrop of red quartzite about 700 ' long. The term petroglyph derives from the Greek words "petra" meaning rock, and "glyphe" meaning carving. Who carved these particular petroglyphs, and when and why, remain good questions.

One theory suggests that they were carved by different peoples inhabiting the region over a period of several centuries. Some of the hunters depicted in the carvings carry atlatls dating to about 3000 BC. Other petroglyphs contain Siouan motifs such as turtles, buffaloes, horned humanoids and thunderbirds, possibly carved as early as 900 AD. One four-legged figure resembling a horse might indicate that these carvings were still being made in the mid-1700s when the Plains Indians obtained horses.

Aboriginal rock art including paintings, carvings and boulder effigies is found throughout the world, but anthropologists caution against trying to read any kind of common meaning into them. Possibly, the humanoid figures at the Jeffers site depict chiefs or shamans. Some of the other designs might have been carved in connection with special rituals, or like petroglyphs found in the western United States, they could be associated with hunting. On the other hand, these petroglyphs may simply have been carved by ancient artists expressing their creative bent.

The Jeffers Petroglyphs are located near the town of Jeffers in northeastern Cottonwood County. From U.S.

highway 71, go east three miles on county road 10, a mile south on county road 2 and 0.3 mile east. (To make things easy, the route is marked.) The site is owned by the Minnesota Historical Society, and it is open to the public daily from May 1 to October 1. A small interpretive center houses exhibits on North American rock art and the region's geology and plant life.

A common sight for nine months of the year in rural Southwestern Minnesota. R. HAMILTON SMITH

in Mankato for more than 100 years. Mankato is the medical center for south-central Minnesota (with a 272-bed hospital and 70 physicians), and Mankato State University is the largest of Minnesota's seven state universities, enrolling 14,000 students. Much to the delight of local fans, the Minnesota Vikings pro football team trains for a month each year in late summer at MSU.

Outside Mankato's Minnesota Valley Regional Library at Front and Main streets, a granite marker commemorates the site of the Indian hangings—the largest legal execution in the United States. In 1987, 125 years after the Dakota War, Minnesota's Governor Rudy Perpich signed a proclamation calling for a "Year of Reconciliation" between the Dakota Indians and the non-Indian community, and an effort is being made to obtain a presidential pardon for the Indians who were executed.

At nearby Kasota, the Vetter Stone Company quarries Minnesota dolomite, used as architectural stone by builders throughout the United States, Canada and overseas. Similar to limestone, dolomite is a stronger, marble-like stone, varying in color from pink and cream to buff and gray. Having undergone metamorphosis by heat and pressure since its formation during the Ordovician Period of the Paleozoic Era, it will take as high a polish as domestic or imported marble. The new Anderson Building at the Los Angeles County Museum of Art is clad in Kasota stone. In Minnesota, pink buff Kasota dolomite will face the new 57-story Norwest Center building in downtown Minneapolis.

Farther west, in Nobles County where there has not been a crop failure since clouds of grasshoppers settled over the entire American frontier in the 1870s, many of the farms are so-called Century Farms, having been in the same family for more than 100 years. With more than 10,000 residents, Worthington is the county seat; it has the area's only shopping mall and two major meat processing plants, Campbell Soup and Swift. But what people usually remember Worthington for is turkeys. Each year, King Turkey Day draws thousands of visitors who cheer the turkeys as they race down a 150-yard course on Main Street.

Farm vacations on working farms are available in southern Minnesota. Group tours of area farms and agribusinesses can also be arranged. Contact: Southern Minnesota Tourism Association, Suite 205, Box 999, 120 South Front Street, Mankato, MN 56001, (507) 345-4517.

southwestern Minnesota's primary trade center. Located in a deep, wooded valley at the junction of the Minnesota and Blue Earth rivers, it was founded by a trio of speculators from St. Paul who put up a log shanty in the dead of a Minnesota winter in 1852. During the next few years, large numbers of immigrant settlers in wagons, covered and uncovered, traveled Minnesota's early military road from Mendota to Mankato on their way to area farmsteads, some of them driving large herds of cattle. Writing in the 1940s and 1950s, children's author Maud Hart Lovelace (born in 1892) drew on her growing-up years in Mankato for her Betsy-Tacy books.

Mankato's economy derives from agri-processing, retailing, health care, education and light industry, with more than 50 manufacturing firms producing everything from sheet metals to fishing equipment. Two large soybean processors sell their products nationally and internationally, and a flour and feed company has prospered

PIPESTONE NATIONAL MONUMENT

Dakota legend has it that the soft red stone that gives its name to the city of Pipestone in southwestern Minnesota is the flesh of the whole Indian nation, drowned in the Flood. The Indians had fled to the higher ground of the Coteau des Prairies as the waters rose, but to no avail. All were drowned, save one maiden who was carried off by a soaring war eagle. Becoming his bride, she bore the children who repopulated the earth.

In another myth, retold in Longfellow's *Song of Hiawatha,* the Great Spirit Gitche Manito calls all the Indian nations together on the quarry's red crags, bidding them to live like brothers. Unless they wash the war paint from their faces and bury their war clubs, Gitche Manito warns them, they will all perish. To bind their truce, he shows them how to break the red stone from the quarry and carve it into peace pipes. Since 1937 the quarry has been part of Pipestone National Monument, a picturesque 283-acre prairie site

where Indians of all tribes can quarry pipestone.

The technical name for pipestone is catlinite, after painter George Catlin. Journeying from New York to Minnesota in the summer of 1836, Catlin traveled up the Minnesota River, sketching the quarry and taking samples of the stone, which he sent to a Boston chemist to be analyzed. Identifying it as a naturally hardened clay composed largely of aluminum silicate and iron impurities, the chemist also coined the word "catlinite."

Pipestone or catlinite is found in a shaly layer only 16″ to 20″ thick, sandwiched between massive layers of a much harder stone, Sioux quartzite (also called red rock, jasper or Sioux Falls granite). Geologists believe that pipestone was originally a clay material and the quartzite was sand that was deposited at the bottom of a sea more than a billion years ago. Other sediments buried these beds deep below the earth's surface, where heat, pressure and chemical action transformed the sand into

quartzite and the clay into pipestone. Later, pressures beneath the surface caused these beds to fold and uplift, and subsequent erosion wore away overlying beds until the pipestone was exposed in some areas.

For several centuries Indians of many tribes traveled great distances on foot to reach the pipestone quarries, considered a sacred place. Pipestone calumets or ceremonial pipes were highly

prized, the Indians using them to solemnize an occasion, to bind an agreement, or for religious ceremonies. For some, the pipe was an altar and the smoke, the incense that carried their prayers to God. An interpretive center at Pipestone National Monument, adjacent to the north side of the city of Pipestone on U.S. 75, houses exhibits. Indian crafts including pipe-making are demonstrated by area Indians.

Sioux quartzite formation at Pipestone National Monument.
JEFF GNASS

MINNESOTA'S HEARTLAND
MAKER OF MYTHS

Lake-studded and forested, central Minnesota is the stuff of legends. Minnesota wit Garrison Keillor picked up on this, locating his mythical Lake Wobegon smack dab in the middle of the state. The only reason that Lake Wobegon is not on any map, he says, is that early government surveyors were less than precise. In fact, they omitted an entire 50 miles of central Minnesota—all of "Mist County."

Four teams of surveyors beginning at the four corners of the state set out for its middle, explains Keillor.

But while the southwestern and northwestern contingents made good time over level terrain, the eastern fellows got slowed down by the woods. When they met a little west of Lake Wobegon, their four quadrants didn't quite fit within the boundaries designated by Congress. So the legislature eventually solved the overlap in the middle by simply eliminating it.

Lake Wobegon showed them all, however, becoming the best-known fictional community in Minnesota. Bleakly ordinary in the present day, the town was founded by 19th-century New England Transcendentalists planning yet another utopia. Now populated mainly by Norwegian Lutherans and German Catholics, most of whom attend either Lake Wobegon Lutheran Church or Our Lady of Perpetual Responsibility, Lake Wobegon points proudly to its one-of-a-kind Statue of the Unknown Norwegian. Thanks to its all-star cast including Doreen of the Chatterbox Cafe, Sister Arvonne, and Ralph of Ralph's Pretty Good Grocery (if Ralph hasn't got it, you probably don't need it), Lake Wobegon is also one good reason Garrison Keillor could afford to move lock, stock and barrel to Denmark.

Long before Keillor was spinning his yarns, Minnesota lumberjacks were telling some of their own. Tall tales grew naturally among the tall timber. The vast north woods gave birth to the biggest and strongest logger of them all—Paul Bunyan. Why, Paul was so big that the top five stories of his house had to be put on hinges to let the moon go by. Deciding to become a lumberjack, Paul hied himself to the Mesabi Range where he scooped up some iron, heated and hammered it, and made himself a proper ax. Able to fell whole forests by the acre, Paul Bunyan was a comic and colossal superman who personified the American brand of exuberance found in the lusty, brawling lumber camps. In the end, he became part and parcel of the Minnesota landscape. Bemidji has a towering statue of Paul Bunyan. Brainerd has the Paul Bunyan Amusement Park.

Locals will tell you that central Minnesota's thousands of lakes are the footprints of Paul Bunyan's blue ox, Babe. But geologists explain the lakes differently. Glaciation created the region's young topography, "moraine terrain" being an apt description of the area. The broad belt of lakes in the west bordering the Glacial Lake Agassiz plain, for instance, is the Alexandria moraine, which extends in a broad arc from Park Rapids to Detroit Lakes, Alexandria, Litchfield and Buffalo. As the last glaciers melted, their dirty ice margins collapsed into bands of kettle lakes and kames (small conical hills of glacial drift). A combination of lakes and wetlands, this is ideal recreational country, attracting fishermen, hunters and hikers. Much of central Minnesota also is prime dairy land with acreage planted to corn, alfalfa and soybeans.

South of the moraines, meltwater spread out in all directions, depositing silt, sand and gravel. These sandy outwash plains are seen near Park Rapids, Brainerd and

Road through autumn woods
R. HAMILTON SMITH

Fishing boat on Mille Lacs Lake. At this now-peaceful lake around 1750, the Ojibwe defeated the Dakota, driving them westward. R. HAMILTON SMITH

Facing page, left: *Newly-emerged dragonfly.* D. CAVAGNARO
Right: *Summer sunset at Willmar Lake—visible evidence of glacial action in this section of Minnesota.* CONNIE WANNER

Above: A springtime carpet of creeping phlox on the floor of a birch forest. DANIEL J. COX

Right: *Paul Bunyan's legend is honored in statues in several Minnesota communities—here at Park Rapids.* GEORGE WUERTHNER

Hunting and fishing bring many visitors into the Heartland region. DANIEL J. COX

Grand Rapids. As glacial ice retreated eastward, swarms of drumlins (elongated hills of glacial drift) were unveiled near Wadena, Brainerd and Pierz. Scattered throughout central Minnesota, serpentine eskers (high sinuous ridges of sand and gravel) mark the pathways of collapsed subsurface glacial drainage tunnels. Itasca and Scenic state parks are good places to view eskers. Except in certain areas, notably the St. Cloud vicinity, central Minnesota has few rock outcrops. Buried under heavy glacial drift, bedrock falls into three primary categories: Lower Precambrian (mostly gneisses), Middle Precambrian stratified rocks and Middle Precambrian plutonic rocks. A broad band of old gneiss, named the McGrath gneiss, extending northeastward from Mille Lacs Lake has been dated as at least 2,700 million years old. Possibly, this is a northern extension of the ancient Minnesota River Valley gneisses; if so, these gneisses are 3,600 million years old. The best-exposed rocks in central Minnesota are plutonic rocks, mostly granites. Both active and abandoned quarries are plentiful in the St. Cloud–Waite Park–Rockville area. St. Cloud granite was used to build St. Paul's Cathedral.

In prehistoric times, central Minnesota was home to the Dakota Indians, but they were subsequently driven westward onto the plains by the Ojibwe. A decisive battle in which the Ojibwe were victorious took place on the southwest shore of Mille Lacs Lake about 1750; thereafter, it was the Ojibwe who inhabited this lake and forest region. On the southwest shore of the lake near Onamia, the Minnesota Historical Society staffs the Mille Lacs Indian Museum, interpreting Dakota and Ojibwe history with life-sized dioramas.

French fur traders were active in the area during the 1600s, and there were fur posts throughout central Minnesota during the entire fur-trade period, most of them located on the principal waterways and Mille Lacs Lake. Several exploring parties ascended the Mississippi in search of its source in the 1800s, the leader of one of these expeditions, Zebulon Pike, naming Little Falls for rapids he encountered in the river. Now a community of 7,250 people, Little Falls was Charles Lindbergh's hometown.

By the 1840s caravans of oxcarts traveling between Red River settlements including Pembina to the northwest and St. Paul and Mendota to the southeast, piled with peltries for the southward journey and loaded with supplies on the way back, trekked established trails across

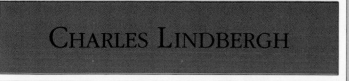

CHARLES LINDBERGH

Minnesota's international hero, Charles Augustus Lindbergh, grew up in Little Falls on a 110-acre farm bordering the Mississippi. The most celebrated aviator in American history, "Lucky Lindy" made headlines around the world when he flew solo and nonstop from New York to Paris in May 1927.

His father, Charles A. Lindbergh, Sr., had come to Minnesota from Sweden with his parents when he was less than a year old. Graduating from the University of Michigan's law school, he became a distinguished lawyer and politician, representing Minnesota in Congress from 1907 to 1917. When his first wife died, leaving him with two young daughters, Charles, Sr., married Evangeline Land, a schoolteacher from Detroit who taught in Little Falls. Their son Charles, born in 1902, was three years old when the family's newly-built three-story mansion on the Little Falls farm burned to the ground. The present Lindbergh house, much less grand, was built on top its charred foundation.

According to Leon Klink, who barnstormed with the famed airman in the mid-1920s, "Slim" Lindbergh cracked up practically everything he flew in those days, once flying smack through the side of a hardware store in Camp Wood, Texas. Prior to flying the Atlantic, Lindbergh earned pocket money as a wingwalker. In 1926 when he set down in a farmer's field because of engine trouble, the farmer put him up for a day, feeding him and giving him a bed. Months later, Lindbergh was sleeping in embassies, feted by kings and queens. He also collected the $25,000 Raymond Orteig prize, waiting since 1919 to be claimed by the first aviator to fly nonstop between Paris and New York.

Appropriately, the main terminal at Minneapolis/St. Paul's International Airport is named for Charles Lindbergh. In Little Falls, the restored Lindbergh farmhouse and an interpretive center are open to the public. Still visible on the sides of a concrete duck pond Lindbergh built the year he graduated from high school is the inscription "Moo Pond." Someone had told him "moo" was the Ojibwe word for "dirt," Charles said, and the pond would be dirty if ducks used it.

Charles Lindbergh was 72 when he died of cancer on Maui, Hawaii, in 1974. In later life, much of his time was devoted to helping the World Wildlife Fund preserve animal species. Much earlier, collaborating with Dr. Alexis Carrel at the Rockefeller Institute for Medical Research in New York, he had helped develop a pump for perfusing living organs. He was outspoken in his belief that the United States should stay out of World War II, but he nonetheless flew 50 combat missions in the South Pacific in 1944, serving with the Navy and Marines as a civilian adviser on fighter planes. In 1954 he received a Pulitzer Prize for his autobiographical work, *The Spirit of St. Louis.*

Charles Lindbergh on tour with the Spirit of St. Louis, *fall 1927.*
WORLD MUSEUM OF MINING, BUTTE, MT

central Minnesota. A decade later, stagecoach lines followed these routes. The city of St. Cloud is located on a former Red River trail.

By 1855 most of central Minnesota had been ceded by the Indians. Loggers came in first, cutting the pine forests along the Mississippi and the Rum rivers, followed by farmers and town builders. The first settlers were easterners, Canadians or settlers from other parts of Minnesota, but they soon were joined by immigrants from Ireland, Scotland, Germany and the Scandinavian countries. Beginning in the late 1860s and continuing through the 1880s—swelling area populations—the Great Northern and the Northern Pacific railroads laid out towns along their lines, including Litchfield, Glenwood, Willmar and Gaylord.

St. Cloud is central Minnesota's largest trade center. With an eye to the beauty of the place, Norwegian Ole

Bergeson squatted in what is now downtown St. Cloud in 1853. That same summer John L. Wilson from Maine paid him $250 for his claim. When he platted the town the next year, Wilson named it for the French city of St. Cloud. Having read Napoleon's biography repeatedly, he had fallen under the spell of the ancient aristocratic city.

Located near what was then the head of navigation on the Mississippi, St. Cloud was a prominent outfitting post for the fur trade in the 1850s and 1860s. Week after week, goods were carried inland, north and west, by long trains of ox or pony carts, while a vast tonnage of furs was packed aboard steamboats for shipment downstream. Railroads eventually absorbed this traffic; the last regular steamboat trip was made upriver in 1874.

Early central Minnesota industry centered almost entirely around area granite quarries. St. Cloud's first quarry opened as a private enterprise in 1868, and there have been as many as 50 quarrying operations in the area at a time, cutting and dressing stone for public and office buildings, churches, bridges and memorials. A must-see replica of a granite quarry at St. Cloud's Heritage Center at 33rd Avenue and 2nd Street South was designed by the people who created Disney's Epcot Center. On Highway 10, Minnesota's first state correctional facility, which opened in 1889, is surrounded by a 22'-high granite wall built by inmates. (Begun in 1905, the wall was completed in the early 1920s.)

Today, with 45,000 residents, St. Cloud is the hub of a fast-growing metropolitan area of more than 100,000 people, many of whom are students. St. Cloud State (home to more than 12,000 undergraduate and graduate students) is located on the west bank of the Mississippi within blocks of downtown. Ten minutes west on Highway 75, the College of St. Benedict is the second largest Catholic women's college in the United States. Fifteen minutes west on I-94 at Collegeville, St. John's University is the oldest liberal arts college in Minnesota. Situated on 2,400 acres of woods and lake, its campus is dominated by an abbey church with a 110-foot bell tower, one of 11 buildings at the school designed by internationally famous architect Marcel Breuer.

Tourism is big business in Minnesota's Heartland. Promotional brochures insist that this region's freshwater fishing is the best in the world. Area waters teem with walleye, muskie, bass, northern pike, trout, crappie, bluegill, catfish and sauger. Northeast of St. Cloud, Mille Lacs Lake, the second largest of Minnesota's lakes (20 miles across with 100 miles of shoreline), draws more walleye anglers than any other state water, and the action is year-round. In winter, the lake is crowded with thousands of shacks and small houses put up by ice fishermen.

Cass and Winnibigoshish are famous Minnesota muskie lakes, but Leech Lake has been more widely publicized. In July 1955, during an unexplained summer flurry now termed "mad muskie days," 140 muskies were taken in a 5^1/2-day period. The largest of them weighed 44 pounds. (Normally, about 150 muskies in the 18-pound range are caught annually at Leech Lake.) Just what caused this fish spree remains a mystery, but the weather was hot, the humidity high, and there had been little wind during the two weeks prior to the amazing catch.

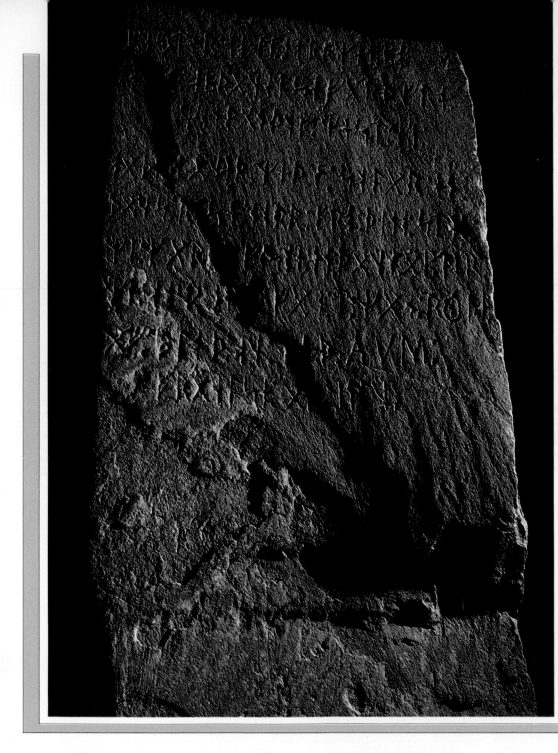

KENSINGTON RUNE STONE

Few puzzles in American history have provoked so much controversy as the Kensington Rune Stone.

In 1898 while clearing land on his farm near Kensington, a Swedish immigrant named Olaf Ohman and his 10-year-old son uncovered a 200-pound stone with runic inscriptions, tangled in the roots of an aspen tree. The message chiseled on it when deciphered read: "8 Swedes and 22 Norwegians on an exploration journey from Vinland westward. We had our camp by 2 rocky islets one day's journey north of this stone. We were out fishing one day. When we came home we found 10 men red with blood and dead. AVM save us from evil. We have 10 men by the sea to look after our ships, 14 days' journey from this island. Year 1362."

Center of controversy, the Kensington Rune Stone.
R. HAMILTON SMITH

According to this, the Vikings had discovered America well before Columbus.

Ohman showed the stone to several neighbors and merchants in Kensington, and word of it leaked to the press, attracting national attention. Needless to say, the stone created a sensation in academic circles, but disappointment soon set in when Norse language experts declared the stone a hoax—and a very recent one at that. No more was said about the stone, and Ohman quietly took it home, where he used it for a granary stepping stone. And that might have been the end of the story, except that the stone came to the attention of historian Hjalmar Holand, interested in pre-Columbian Viking explorations, who acquired it from Ohman in 1907.

Although European runologists pointed out that a number of the symbols on the stone were unknown in 1362, Holand argued that the stone recorded a religious expedition headed by Baron Paul Knutson, who had been charged by Magnus Erickson, the militant Catholic ruler of Norway and Sweden, with bringing fallen-away Catholics in far-off Greenland back to the Church. Not finding the errant colonists in Greenland, Knutson continued his search on the North American continent, eventually reaching what is now Douglas County in Minnesota. Those men who carved the rune stone, Holand said, abandoned any hope of ever seeing Norway again and remained in the wilderness. Venturing west of the Red River, they intermarried with the Mandan Indians in central North Dakota.

Holand reached a wide audience with his book: *A Study In Pre-Columbian American History,* in 1932, and the rune stone was subsequently exhibited at the Smithsonian Institution, where one official described it as "probably the most important archaeological object yet found in North America." *National Geographic* covered the exhibition and pictured the curator of archaeology with the stone, commenting that "later studies indicate that it was carved by white men who had traveled far into North America long before Columbus's first voyage." That was endorsement enough for many people, and the stone was treated with new respect when it returned to Minnesota. Holand had sold it to a group of businessmen in Alexandria, 23 miles northeast of Kensington, and the city constructed an area historical museum to enshrine it. So at last, thanks to Holand, rumors of a hoax had been put to rest. But had they?

Most historians now agree that the stone is a fake, chiseled by amateurs. Minnesota historian Theodore Blegen also found it an amazing coincidence that the stone was found by a Scandinavian, in an area peopled by Scandinavian immigrants, at a time when there was tremendous interest in Viking explorations of North America. Ohman and his minister, Sven Fogelblad, it turns out, were keenly interested in Viking history, and they had books which would have helped them carve the inscription. Further, they were both known to be fun-loving, which only adds credence to the local rumor, circulated immediately after the find, that the whole thing was a prank, staged to confound academicians.

Alexandria, the county seat of Douglas County, still treasures the Kensington Rune Stone, and it also boasts a granite replica, five times its size, erected in 1951 at the east entrance to the city. Authentic or not, the Rune Stone is an apt memorial to Douglas County pioneers, whose descendants can appreciate a good joke.

Park Rapids—central Minnesota is dotted with small towns as well as with lakes. R. HAMILTON SMITH

Numerous former lumber towns in central Minnesota have become vacation meccas. Built by the Northern Pacific Railroad in 1870, Brainerd is a good example. Named for the railroad president's wife, Ann Eliza Brainerd Smith, Brainerd boomed as a lumber town before the turn of the century. (Eight thousand lumberjacks once quenched their thirst in its 36 saloons.) Now a northern gateway to thousands of lakes and resorts, the town depends upon tourism. There are more than 460 fishing lakes of all shapes and sizes within a 30-mile radius of Brainerd. Breezy Point on Big Pelican Lake is one of Minnesota's best-known resorts, with housekeeping cabins, condominiums and motels. Open all year, it offers golf, tennis, fishing, boating, swimming, cross-country skiing and snowmobiling.

Bemidji is a second early lumber town *cum* tourist haven. Located in choice lake and forest country on the shore of 12-mile-long Lake Bemidji, it appeals to fishermen, hunters and hikers alike. Some 1 million acres of land and water area in this region are in public hands, providing almost unlimited recreational opportunities in

Hometown heartland—this at Wilmar. CONNIE WANNER

state parks and forests, national forest lands and wildlife management areas. Fishing in area lakes is a year-round proposition, and Bemidji is located within the Mississippi Flyway, affording excellent waterfowl hunting. Large numbers of sportsmen also come this way to hunt grouse and whitetailed deer. Each year in January, Bemidji hosts the top sled dog race in the lower 48 states, the 16-mile course being run in the open on Lake Bemidji.

At Sauk Center, in the middle of the lakes region, townspeople have made peace with Sinclair Lewis in a big way. When Governor Orville Freeman proclaimed Sinclair Lewis Year in 1960, marking the 40th anniversary of the publication of *Main Street*—the novel that had scandalized the town—Sauk Center renamed its major thoroughfare "The Original Main Street," and also named a city park for Lewis. On Sinclair Lewis Avenue (formerly Third Avenue) the Sinclair Lewis Boyhood Home has been restored through a joint effort by the Sinclair Lewis Foundation and the Minnesota Historical Society, and the Bryant Public Library on Main Street houses the Sinclair Lewis Museum.

So much for bruised feelings.

LAKE ITASCA
HEADWATERS OF THE MISSISSIPPI

America's greatest river begins unpretentiously in a small Minnesota lake named Itasca, cupped in low hills, a hundred miles from the Canadian border. Hidden in a labyrinth of northern Minnesota lakes and marshes, its true source remained a mystery for three centuries after Hernando de Soto discovered the lower Mississippi in 1541. In the meantime, numerous explorers claimed to have found its headwaters elsewhere.

One of the first of these was Zebulon Pike (for whom Pike's Peak in Colorado is named), who understandably identified the wrong lake in 1806, having located it in midwinter when Minnesota's topography is hidden beneath ice and snow. Next came Lewis Cass, governor of Michigan Territory, who paddled northward with 40 men to within a hundred miles of Itasca and convinced himself that the Mississippi flowed from the lake now named for him, Cass Lake.

The most flamboyant of the would-be discoverers was Giacomo Constantino Beltrami, an uncongenial political exile from Venice who arrived in America in 1823 and booked passage on the *Virginia*, the first steamer to ascend the Mississippi as far as the Falls of St. Anthony. At Fort Snelling, Beltrami attached himself to an American expedition headed by Major Stephen Long, commissioned to survey the border between Canada and the United States. But the army officer and the Italian didn't get on well together. Having come as far as Pembina on the Red River, Beltrami separated from the expedition, secured an interpreter and Ojibwe guides, and set out on his own.

His troubles were only beginning. The interpreter soon turned back, and Beltrami's party was ambushed by Dakota Indians. The Ojibwe then abandoned him, and the Italian was left pulling his birchbark canoe upriver (because he hadn't learned to maneuver it alone), his

78

possessions protected from continuing rain by a red silk umbrella. In the end, having found a mixed-blood man to guide him, Beltrami concluded that the Mississippi originated in a lake 12 miles north of Bemidji, a lake he christened Lake Julia for a deceased lady friend. Returning triumphantly downstream to Fort Snelling, thinking that he ranked beside world-famed explorers, Beltrami boarded a steamer for New Orleans. He hadn't found the source of the Mississippi, but he was still the first man to travel virtually its entire length.

Henry Rowe Schoolcraft was a more modest man. He had accompanied the earlier Cass expedition, but he felt that it had stopped short of the headwaters. Twelve years later in 1832, employed as an Indian agent at Sault Ste. Marie, Michigan, Schoolcraft headed a government-funded expedition into the Minnesota region for the expressed purposes of mediating intertribal conflicts and inoculating the Indians against smallpox. Personally, Schoolcraft had more on his mind. Arriving at Cass Lake, he took a small detachment and paddled upstream, in three days reaching the body of water he named Lake Itasca. There was precious little time for fanfare. Needing

to get on with his official objectives, Schoolcraft spent only two hours at the lake. The men raised a flag on the lakeshore, fired a volley, then paddled back downstream. The report Schoolcraft later filed with the Indian Office described his discovery of the Mississippi's true source in two brief sentences. Coined by Schoolcraft, the word Itasca derives from two Latin words: *veritas* meaning truth, and *caput* meaning head.

Few white men visited the area in the next 50 years, until loggers heard of its virgin pine forests. Even as loggers denuded the timberlands, conservationists led by Jacob Brower fought to protect them, advocating a state park. Recognizing that Lake Itasca lies near the transition zone between conifer and prairie communities, early park supporters sought to preserve this unique ecotone of forest and prairie. When Itasca State Park was established in 1891, Brower was named park commissioner, though he was powerless to stop the logging which continued on privately-owned property within Itasca's boundaries until 1919.

Itasca is one of the largest of Minnesota's 64 state parks, encompassing more than 32,000 acres. Much of it is heavily wooded and it contains more than a hundred

lakes. There are two prehistoric Indian occupation sites within the park, and paved roads lead to a research station, an inn and a museum. Yearly, thousands of pilgrims seek out the headwaters whence the Mississippi begins

its 2,348-mile journey to the gulf. Few can resist the impulse to cross the tiny stream. To do so takes only six paces on stones placed in the water.

Lake Itasca, whence flows the Mississippi. BOB EIKUM

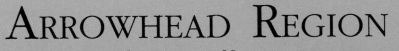

CHAPTER
8

ARROWHEAD REGION
SIREN OF THE NORTH

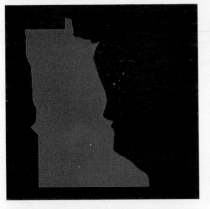

Above: Catch of smelt on Lake Superior fishing boat. DANIEL & JULIE COX
Right: *Sunrise on Lake Superior.* TOM TILL ***Facing page:*** *Grand Portage Bay, Lake Superior.* DANIEL J. COX

In 1924 when a local civic group held an international contest to name this region, an observant Pittsburgh man noted that it was shaped roughly like an arrowhead. His suggestion that it be called the "Minnesota Arrowhead" won the contest, and the name has stuck.

A land of superlatives, the Minnesota Arrowhead has more than 4,000 lakes including Lake Superior, the world's largest freshwater lake. It contains the state's richest iron ore deposits, its only three-way watershed and

its most rugged topography. Both Minnesota's lowest and highest elevations occur in northeastern Minnesota. Lake Superior is 602' above sea level; a few miles inland, Eagle Mountain in the Misquah Hills rises 2,301' above sea level.

Delighting even neophyte geologists, northeastern Minnesota has more rock outcrops than any other part of the state, and it displays some of the world's best exposures of Precambrian rocks, dating to 2.7 billion years ago. These well-studied rocks include the Vermilion district's volcanic-sedimentary greenstone belt, seen to particular advantage in and near Ely; three great batholiths: the Giant's Range (recently developed as a ski area), the Vermilion and the Saganaga; a portion of the Precambrian sea basin in which the Mesabi range's world-famous Biwabik Iron Formation was deposited; well exposed continental lava flows along the shore of Lake Superior; and the Duluth Complex of gabbroic rocks, one of the world's largest mafic intrusions, as well as a major reservoir of copper and nickel, which extends in a broad arc from Duluth to Ely and back to Lake Superior at Grand Portage.

Because it lies so far north, this area's glacial history differs from that of southern Minnesota. While glaciers repeatedly advanced and retreated to the south, this region generally remained under ice, subject to erosion rather than glacial deposition. Glacial drift is noticeably sparse in wide areas, but glacial abrasion and quarrying are readily seen in the form of boulders, polished and striated rock outcrops and sculpted rock lake basins. In contrast to southern and western lakes that usually formed in glacial drift, most of northeastern Minnesota's lakes are ponded in solid bedrock. Lake Superior, a remnant of Glacial Lake Duluth that was formed by glacial meltwater, occupies a deep basin carved by earlier subglacial erosion.

A rare and beautiful land of lakes and forests, the Arrowhead embraces Superior National Forest, the largest national forest east of the Mississippi, encompassing more than 2 million acres. Within Superior National Forest, the Boundary Waters Canoe Area (BWCA) stretches 150 miles along the border between the United States and Canada. Part of the Wilderness Preservation System, the BWCA takes in more than 1 million acres, containing several thousand portage-linked lakes and streams, interspersed with islands, woods and crags. (On the Canadian side of the border, sister to the BWCA, Ontario's Quetico Provincial Park is a similar million-acre wilderness area.)

Adjoining Superior National Forest at its westernmost point, Voyageurs National Park comprises another 219,000 acres of pristine border lake country. Together, the BWCA and Voyageurs National Park span the famed Voyageurs Highway between Lake Superior and Lake of the Woods where visitors can canoe, portage and camp in the spirit of the French Canadian voyageurs. Two hundred years ago, this fur traders' water route was so well

Birch stand. R. HAMILTON SMITH

known that the 1783 treaty ending the American Revolution made it a portion of the new international boundary. Preserved in this shimmering lake and stream wilderness are the same resources that spurred this continent's first major industry.

The fur trade relied on three key ingredients: water highways, plentiful fur-bearing animals (primarily beavers) and birchbark canoes. The boundless forests provided the makings for the latter. Truly an amazing example of environmental adaptation, canoes made of birchbark, cedar boughs and cedar or spruce root bindings sealed with pitch were developed by woodland Indians, but readily exploited by early European explorers and furmen. Besides being lightweight (which counted for much on long portages), birchbark canoes were easy to navigate and quickly repaired with available materials. One historian has described the fur trade as a vast empire held together by nothing stronger than birchbark.

By the time American colonists 1,000 miles to the east signed the Declaration of Independence at Philadelphia in 1776, Minnesota's northern wilderness already could brag of a bustling fur trading port at Grand Portage. Strategically located at the east end of a nine-mile trail linking Lake Superior with the interconnected border lakes, Grand Portage is one of North America's most important fur trade sites. First claimed by Frenchmen, Grand Portage passed to British hands with the close of the French and Indian War. In its heyday, from the 1770s until 1803, the outpost was headquarters for the North West Company's far-flung fur trade empire that stretched 3,000 miles from Montreal to Fort Chipewyan on Lake Athabaska in the northwestern wilderness.

July was the busiest month of the year at Grand Portage when as many as a thousand white men, including the firms' partners from Montreal, the winterers (voyageurs who wintered in the country west of Lake Superior), the pork eaters (canoemen who paddled between Montreal and Grand Portage), and hundreds of Indian men, women and children gathered for the annual rendezvous. Accounts were settled, trade goods from Montreal repacked for western posts, and furs from the interior sorted and packed for Montreal and European markets. When the business at hand was completed, the celebrating began, the brightly-garbed voyageurs swinging Indian women to the lively music of violins, flutes and bagpipes.

SOFT GOLD

It has been quite a come-down for the Minnesota beaver. Although still among the state's ranking furbearers, the beaver has become the number-one nuisance animal hereabouts, building dams that flood farm fields, timber stands, roads, trout streams and lakeshore property.

It was the beaver, you remember, that brought the first Frenchmen seeking "soft gold" (beaver pelts) to what is now Minnesota. But beaver nearly disappeared altogether from this region during the waning days of the fur trade, becoming so uncommon that in 1909 the state legislature declared them a protected species. For the next 30 years, trapping was prohibited.

This is all in the past. Having made a remarkable come-back, beaver numbers in Minnesota currently approximate those of the early fur trade years; the reasons are managed trapping seasons and hospitable habitat created by logging and burning. These latter activities promote the growth of aspen trees, which beavers prefer to any other food.

Coping with the present overpopulation, Minnesota's Department of Natural Resources now encourages trappers to take all the beavers they can. Trapping is not very profitable in the 1980s—a beaver pelt brings only about $16—but Minnesota trappers sell about 60,000 beaver pelts annually.

Above: Beaver building dam at edge of pond. Mud to "mortar" the house is taken from the bottom. DANIEL J. COX
Far left: Preparing to destroy a beaver dam. STEVE KAUFMAN
Left: Beaver dam and pond. D. CAVAGNARO

Ship in port at Duluth, whose harbor has determined its history.
R. HAMILTON SMITH

ence Center, a hotel and campground complex at Grand Portage that is tribally owned. The reservation also takes in the original site of the North West Company post, now Grand Portage National Monument. Administered by the U.S. Park Service, its rebuilt stockade, great hall, kitchen, canoe warehouse and dock—interpreted by costumed guides—take visitors back in time to 1797.

One hundred fifty miles south of Grand Portage on Lake Superior, with 90,000 residents, Duluth is Minnesota's third largest city. Long and crescent-shaped, hugging sheer granite cliffs that drop precipitously to the cold blue lake, it occupies the most picturesque location of any city in the state. More importantly, it is a world port, with one of the largest natural harbors in North America. Destined by its geography to be a crossroads for ship and rail traffic in the heart of the continent, the town has nonetheless boomed and gone bust more than once.

In 1854 rumors of immense copper deposits along the North Shore triggered a land rush that was short-lived. The national panic in 1857 abruptly closed down the fledgling town. A decade later, reports of iron ore and gold-bearing quartz at Lake Vermilion brought thousands of gold-seekers into the area, and Jay Cooke ensured Duluth's prosperity by making the city the Lake Superior terminus for his Lake Superior and Mississippi Railroad (later part of the Northern Pacific system). Or so it seemed. When Jay Cooke failed in 1873, the sky caved in on Duluth a second time. Banks folded, real estate values plummeted, and the population dwindled from about 5,000 to 1,300.

Marshalling its resources, Duluth bounced back quickly this time, the twin reasons being lumber and grain. Moving westward from New England and Michigan, lumber barons saw their future in the northern forests; Duluth's sawmills helped make Minnesota the world's largest producer of white pine. At the same time, vast prairie grasslands to the west had been planted to grain. Elevators and warehouses sprang up along the docks and, by 1886, with its population swelled to 26,000, Duluth was handling more grain than Chicago. Four years later when the Merritts opened the Mesabi Range, Duluth was the fifth largest seaport in the United States. As a transportation hub and the gateway to the mining districts, the city filled with mining company officers, engineers, consultants and lawyers. Lumbering was winding

British troops were stationed at Grand Portage during the Revolutionary War. Even after the United States emerged the winner, the North West Company did not move its operations across the Canadian border to Fort William until forced to in 1803. There the competition from the rival Hudson's Bay Company proved too stiff, and the North West Company was absorbed by that firm in 1821. Back on the American side of the border, John Jacob Astor operated a fur post and fishing enterprise at Grand Portage into the 1840s. By that time, all remains of the North West Company fort had disappeared.

In 1854 a treaty signed with the Ojibwe at La Pointe, Wisconsin ceded most of the Arrowhead country to the United States and one of Minnesota's seven Ojibwe reservations was created at Grand Portage. Occupying more than 44,000 acres at the northeastern tip of Minnesota, the reservation has a population of about 200 Indians, many of whom work in the Grand Portage Lodge and Confer-

Clockwise from upper left:
Cross-country skiers on the North Shore Trail.
Duluth's famed aerial lift bridge.
Lutsen Lodge on Lake Superior at Lutsen.
Sunset in the Boundary Waters Canoe Area near Ely.
R. HAMILTON SMITH PHOTOS

ARTIST OF THE WILDERNESS

FRANCIS LEE JAQUES

Francis Lee Jaques stands alone among Minnesota wildlife painters. No one before or after him has painted just like Jaques. He knew wildlife and he knew its habitat. Even so, he prided himself on never being a feather painter. The effect or illusion was what mattered to him, not unnecessary scientific detail. A good painting must be technically correct, he believed, but also artistically interpreted. "I never intended to produce giant Kodachromes," he once explained.

His formal schooling virtually nil, Jaques (pronounced *jay-quees*) achieved a world-wide reputation as a museum artist for his diorama backgrounds, particularly those at the American Museum of Natural History in New York. He was lionized in his lifetime for his superb easel paintings, which ran the gamut from all manner of waterfowl to big game animals. Collaborating with well known authors (including his wife, Florence Page Jaques, and their close friend, Sigurd Olson), he also illustrated 40 books, many of them with his distinctive black-and-white scratchboard drawings.

Born in 1887, Lee grew up on a farm in Kansas, where he spent his free time hunting ducks and geese in nearby creeks and marshland. Taken with the beauty of the birds he bagged, he routinely sketched them as well. "When I was young, I drew constantly, though I had no idea I might ever do this as an occupation," he wrote. Lee was 16 when his family moved to a farm north of Aitkin, and wintertimes, Lee helped his father cut timber that they floated downriver to sawmills in the spring. The reason he later painted trees as well as he did, he said, was because he had taken so many of them apart.

Learning to mount birds and game animals, Lee opened a taxidermy shop in Aitkin, and he operated it for nine years. He also worked several years as a fireman (stoking steam engines) on railroads servicing the iron-ore mines in northern Minnesota. Railroading was a lifelong fascination, and it introduced him to Minnesota's extraordinary canoe country. On a trip to an iron mine near Ely, he had his first glimpse of the most beautiful pine forests he ever had seen. "It was one of those times or events which change the rest of your life and you know it," he said. When he later married writer Florence Page, the pair honeymooned in Minnesota's Boundary Waters Canoe Area. An account of that trip, their first book, *Canoe Country,* has become a Minnesota classic.

Jaques was nearly 40 when he landed a job as a museum artist at the American Museum of Natural History in New York. During the next 18 years, he painted 80 large diorama backgrounds, traveling to the far corners of the world for his research. Beginning in the 1940s, he also painted more than a dozen Minnesota backgrounds for the James Ford Bell Museum of Natural History at the University of Minnesota—and no work could have made him happier. Minnesota was the part of the world he knew best and preferred to all others. His sketches for the wolf diorama were made near the mouth of the Baptism River on Lake Superior, those for the moose group at Gunflint Lake and for the elk, at Inspiration Point in the Leaf Hills in the west-central part of Minnesota.

In 1953, moving to Minnesota to stay, Lee and Florence built one of the first homes at North Oaks, formerly railroad builder Jim Hill's summer farm on the outskirts of St. Paul. The house was a showcase for some of Lee's finest easel paintings. (You could buy one of his oils in those years for $500; today a Jaques painting, when you can find one for sale, carries a hefty five-figure price tag.) Turning to nostalgic themes, he produced several semi-autobiographical paintings; Florence's favorite pictured a young boy sitting beside his team of horses and plow, gazing skyward at a great flat-topped cloud. He also thoroughly enjoyed what he termed his red boxcar period, painting many railroad scenes. Downstairs, on the walkout level of their modest house, Lee built a superb miniature railroad he called the Great North Road.

Following his death at the age of 81 in 1969, Florence wrote *Francis Lee Jaques: Artist of the Wilderness World,* her husband's biography, lavishly illustrated with his paintings and drawings. Lee's *Great North Road* was dismantled and shipped to Duluth where it is displayed in the city's historic depot. Florence also saw to establishing the Jaques Gallery at the James Ford Bell Museum, the core collection being paintings from the Jaques' home at North Oaks.

Facing page: CARIBOU ON ICE. *Oil on canvas by Francis Lee Jaques, 30" x 36", late 1940s.* JAMES FORD BELL MUSEUM OF NATURAL HISTORY, UNIVERSITY OF MINNESOTA, MINNEAPOLIS

Above: Ore boats at Two Harbors Port.

Right: Split Rock Lighthouse on Lake Superior, which operated from 1909 to 1969, allows today's visitors to understand the peril of Great Lakes navigation before radar.

DANIEL J. COX PHOTOS

down, but iron-ore mining brought new prosperity to Duluth.

Duluth's history has been that of her extraordinary harbor. As early as 1857, Duluth citizens formed the Minnesota Point Ship Canal Company to transform Superior Bay into "the largest, most easily accessible and safest harbor" on the Great Lakes. Their plans became a reality in 1870 when Jay Cooke backed the digging of a canal across the long narrow sandbar called Minnesota Point. Together with Wisconsin Point, a somewhat shorter

sandbar, Minnesota Point protects the Duluth harbor from the open waters of Lake Superior.

Across the bay in Wisconsin, Superior residents fought the new canal every step of the way, fearing it would ruin the harbor's less practical natural entrance between Minnesota Point and Wisconsin Point, but to no avail. Although the protestors finally obtained a federal injunction to halt the canal's construction, all Duluth turned out to dig and shovel, completing the canal before the legal papers arrived. Subsequently, the federal government assumed control of both the canal and harbor; in 1893 it became the Duluth-Superior Harbor.

Since completion of the St. Lawrence Seaway in 1959, ships flying flags from more than 30 countries have entered the Duluth-Superior harbor through the Duluth Ship Canal to be loaded with iron ore, coal, grain and Canadian crude oil. Stretching 2,304' into Lake Superior, the Duluth Mesabi and Iron Range ore-loading docks can be seen from an observation platform at the end of Frontage Road in Duluth. These are the world's longest ore docks. But the Aerial Bridge that spans the harbor entrance at Canal Park is Duluth's number-one tourist attraction. Built in 1905, it is the largest and fastest lift bridge in the world, rising 138 feet in 55 seconds. I still can remember the special childhood thrill of watching it go up and down for ore boats coming into the harbor.

I was three years old when my father was transferred to Duluth from St. Paul in the 1940s to open a branch office for Blue Cross, and my family lived there five years. Part of that time, we lived just around the corner from Minnesota's Nobel Prize-winning novelist, Sinclair Lewis, who had earned the everlasting enmity of many of his former neighbors in Sauk Center by depicting them unfavorably in *Main Street*. Having come to Duluth to write *Cass Timberlane*, Lewis lived at 2601 East 2nd Street, in a magnificent 30-room brick Tudor mansion with a third-floor ballroom and a bowling alley in the basement, that he purchased in 1945 for $15,000 (one tenth what it had cost to build it in 1912). My own cherished memory of that house goes back to one Halloween evening when my brother and two sisters and I knocked on the author's door. Invited in by his maid to join an ongoing party, we bobbed for apples with other neighborhood children in the third floor ballroom.

In Duluth, Lewis, who had shed two wives by that time, met Judge Mark Nolan, who proved an invaluable character study for his judge in *Cass Timberlane* and a great friend besides. Doing his research, Lewis was in Nolan's courtroom at 10 o'clock sharp each morning, and he also followed Nolan on his circuit cases. His own car was in storage due to wartime gas rationing, so Lewis hired taxi owner Asa Lyons as his chauffeur. The setting for *Cass Timberlane* was the tiny village of Arthyde, about 60 miles southwest of Duluth, which Lewis superimposed on Duluth to produce his fictional metropolis, Grand Republic. Lewis's neighbors often saw him working outside

Above: Duluth's aerial lift bridge with passing ship. R. HAMILTON SMITH
Left: Sailboats on Lake Superior near Duluth. DANIEL J. COX

89

IRON GIANTS AND RED GOLD

For sheer drama, the saga of iron ore mining in Minnesota is unmatched. It begins with the Ojibwe tale of a giant hero who hunted wild animals with granite boulders plucked from the earth. His name was "Mesabi," and he afterwards slept for many generations in the Lake Superior country. Once discovered and exploited by iron men and eastern tycoons, this sleeping giant birthed an industry of gigantic proportions that helped make America a world power. The rich ore seemed limitless at first, but when it seemed to be bottoming out, new techniques were developed to utilize the low-grade taconite. Iron-ore mining was always a jackpot game. At stake were Minnesota's three great iron ranges: the Vermilion, the Mesabi and the Cuyuna.

While early prospectors searched the Lake Vermilion region in vain for gold, they overlooked the valuable iron ore deposits right under their feet. Henry H. Eames, Minnesota's first state geologist, found iron ore 50' to 60' thick near Vermilion Lake in the 1860s, but he wasn't much interested in it. "To hell with iron," he told a companion. "It's gold we're after." There was nothing save fool's gold at Lake Vermilion, but Minnesota's rich iron-ore deposits ultimately were brought to the attention of a wealthy Pennsylvanian, Charlemagne Tower. Buying 20,000 acres of land in northeastern Minnesota, Tower opened Minnesota's first iron-ore mine on the Vermilion Range on July 31, 1884. Perhaps dreading the onset of Minnesota winter, the mine's manager wistfully named it the Soudan, calling up warmer African climes.

Tower brought in experienced Cornish and Swedish miners to work the Soudan, putting up houses for them and their families nearby; the town of Tower was established as a trade center for the fast-growing population. Charlemagne Tower built the Duluth and Iron Range Railroad to transport the iron ore to Two Harbors on Lake Superior. (His first wooden dock was located on the site of the modern steel and concrete ore docks seen from Paul Van Hoven Park in Two Harbors.) During peak production years in the 1890s, the Soudan Mine employed 1,800 workers, but by then Tower had sold his holdings for a tidy profit. When United States Steel Corporation was formed in 1901, the Soudan came under its Oliver Iron Mining Division. Continuing in operation until 1962, the Soudan is now a National Historic Landmark. Blasted out of solid bedrock, it never needed supporting timbers, and it is the only mine in the world that offers underground tours. Former miners act as guides, taking visitors underground 2,341' to the mine's 27th level.

By 1890 the boom that Charlemagne Tower started had led to discovery of fabulous ore deposits at Ely, and no fewer than 284 mining companies had been incorporated. But the boom was only beginning. That same year the Merritts roused the sleeping Mesabi giant, the largest iron deposit the world has ever known. Duluth pioneer Lewis H. Merritt had been a disappointed gold seeker who returned home with a lump of iron ore. Years later, when it turned out that Merritt had turned his back on a fortune, his four sons and their four nephews took up the search for iron ore, continuing their explorations while they worked as timber cruisers for 16 years.

After spending a small fortune drilling for iron ore, the Merritts struck pay dirt at the site of their famous Mountain Iron Mine near Virginia. Although covered by heavy forest, the ore was much closer to the surface than they had ever dreamed possible, finally showing itself when a heavy wagon wheel cut into the red, powdery material. Unlike typically hard iron ores, it was located in surface deposits where it could be scooped from open pits. Between 1892 and the time it closed in 1956, the Mountain Iron Mine shipped more than 48 million tons of iron ore.

Fast on the heels of the Merritts' discovery at Mountain Iron, high-grade ore deposits were found at Biwabik, Eveleth, Hibbing and as far west as Coleraine. The Merritts became Minnesota's best-known pioneer iron men, helping shape the industry, but their story did not end happily. In the midst of the 1893 depression, while attempting to build a railroad to transport iron ore to Duluth, they overextended themselves and lost both the railroad and their ore properties to John D. Rockefeller. Success in iron mining hinged on heavy capitalization, and small-time operators, including the Merritts, soon were counted out. For the most part, with a few exceptions including James J. Hill, the iron magnates were not Minnesota men.

His appetite whetted, John D. Rockefeller continued gobbling up iron-ore mining companies, shipping raw ore to blast furnaces in the East via his own railroad and steamships. Meanwhile, Henry W. Oliver of Pittsburgh convinced steel king Andrew Carnegie to back his Oliver Mining Company, and in 1896 the Carnegie-Oliver combine leased most of the Rockefeller mines, Rockefeller stipulating that all ores be shipped on his railroad, ships and barges. In the end, J. Pierpont Morgan got into the act, acquiring the Carnegie properties for more than $500 million in 1901, before adding Rockefeller's Mesabi holdings and ore carriers for another $90 million. Christened United States Steel, Morgan's new company was a behemoth of ore mines and ore vessels, steel plants, coal lands, blast furnaces, railroads and other properties with a capital value of almost $1.5 billion. U.S. Steel was this country's first billion-dollar enterprise.

Minnesota's third great iron range, the Cuyuna, is unique in that its iron ore is rich in manganese. During World War I when American imports of manganese were cut back, nine tenths of the nation's manganese, used to manufacture steel, came from Cuyuna mines. The name Cuyuna has a Indian ring to it, but the range is named for the surveyor who discovered it in 1904, Cuyler Adams, and his dog Una, who accompanied him on his explorations. Located in Crow Wing County, the range begot the mining villages of Trommald, Riverton, Manganese, Cuyuna, Crosby and Ironton, the last two surviving as good-sized towns. With new mines opened into the 1950s, the Cuyuna was mined by both open-pit and underground methods. Only one mine currently is being worked to obtain manganiferous iron ore, but the Cuyuna represents this nation's greatest reserves of manganese.

All told, more than 400 Minnesota mines produced in excess of 6 billion tons of iron ore between 1884 and 1980; about 94 percent of this total came from the Mesabi Range. Most of Minnesota's high-grade iron ore deposits have been depleted, but the state still has enormous taconite reserves. Presently, taconite shipments account for three quarters of Minnesota's iron ore exports, with the state continuing to produce more than half of this country's iron ore. Discoveries of iron ore in Australia and elsewhere have greatly increased available ore supplies, however, with the result that Minnesota's share of the current world market is something less than eight percent.

While early miners knew about taconite, it was only after mine owners realized that high-grade ores would one day be exhausted that anyone considered its commercial possibilities. Sometimes called the world's hardest rock, taconite is the mother rock of the iron range, extending in a diagonal band for 110 miles across northeastern Minnesota. Although relatively low in iron content, it contains pockets of richer iron ore (which have been compared to raisins in a cake). Beginning in the 1910s, scientist Edward W. Davis at the University of Minnesota spent more than

four decades developing a taconite pelleting process. What this one man really did was to guarantee that Minnesota iron mining will continue indefinitely into the future.

In 1955 Reserve Mining Company produced this country's first commercial taconite pellets at its new plant, named for Davis, at Silver Bay. Simply put, taconite is first broken into small pieces, than crushed to a flour-like consistency. Giant magnets extract usable ore particles, and these particles are mixed with a binding clay to form marble-sized pellets that are baked. Ironically, taconite pellets have substantially increased the capacities of blast furnaces, roughly doubling the amount of steel a furnace can produce compared to its output using natural ore. Consequently, the value of natural ore remaining in the ground has greatly declined.

The world's largest open-pit mine, the Hull-Rust-Mahoney at Hibbing, about 1940.
MINNESOTA HISTORICAL SOCIETY

on the raised front patio of his home, but he had had the stairs to it walled up lest the postman or anyone else disturb his thoughts. This left the only entrance to his home in the rear.

Sinclair Lewis's home was only one of many extravagant residences of its era. Duluth was no stranger to the City Beautiful movement that had come to town in the early 1900s. Led by Chicago architect Daniel Hudson Burnham, the City Beautiful movement decreed that the center of a great city demanded beautiful monumental buildings. Burnham's firm designed Duluth's classic Civic Center (composed of the St. Louis County Courthouse flanked by the Duluth City Hall and the Federal Building) and also the 16-story reinforced concrete and steel Alworth Building. In Duluth's residential areas, newly-rich entrepreneurs hired the nation's finest architects to design their personal dwellings. The city's eastern suburban area, where Sinclair Lewis lived, presents more architecturally remarkable residences than does any comparable area in the Twin Cities.

Among them is Glensheen, a 39-room Jacobean-style manor house on $7^{1}/_{2}$ acres of Lake Superior lakeshore. It was built in 1905 at a cost of $864,000 by Elisabeth Congdon's father, attorney Chester Adgate Congdon who had made a fortune in the iron mining business. In 1972 Elisabeth Congdon allowed the house to be used in a film starring Patty Duke, *You'll Like My Mother.* The film concerns a young widow who visits her mother-in-law in a family mansion. What the young woman doesn't know is that her mother-in-law has been murdered and that the woman impersonating her is one of the murderers.

Glensheen, a Jacobean mansion on Lake Superior in Duluth, was built in 1905 by attorney Chester Adgate Congdon, and now is open to the public. CHARLES J. JOHNSTON

Glensheen's brochures don't mention it but this mansion now belonging to the University of Minnesota, which conducts public house tours, was the scene of Minnesota's most publicized murders. On the night of June 27, 1977, after bludgeoning nurse Velma Pietila to death with a candlestick, Roger Caldwell smothered 83-year-old Duluth heiress Elisabeth Congdon in her bed with a pink satin pillow.

Commercial fishermen emptying smelt into boat bins. DANIEL J. COX

Duluth has been in yet another economic downslide in recent times. In 1982 the *Wall Street Journal* named Duluth one of the 10 most financially distressed cities in the nation. Iron ore and grain exports were down, the city had a 16 percent unemployment rate, and almost 2,000 homes were for sale. You only had to drive through

its aging central business district to see that Duluth was in the doldrums.

A lesser city finally might have thrown in the towel, but not Duluth. Together, City Hall and the Greater Downtown Council formed a public-private partnership that decided to look seriously at tourism and revitalize the city. Giving downtown streets a turn-of-the-century look, main thoroughfares have been paved with 3.5 million bricks, storefronts renovated, and wrought-iron lampposts installed. Stressing the city's maritime image, the biggest changes are occurring on the waterfront where Canal Park is being upgraded, a two-mile Lakewalk built, and a hotel, convention center and arena complex constructed.

To boot, the ore boat *William A. Irvin,* the retired flagship of the U.S. Steel fleet, now does duty as a museum in a downtown slip. Opened in July 1986, the *Irwin* attracted 70,000 tourists in its first season.

The Arrowhead's leading cultural entity, Duluth's renovated 1892 Norman chateau-style railroad Union Depot houses three museums, including one of this country's largest railroad museums, four performing arts groups and an art institute. Across the street, the city's striking new public library has been patterned after an ore boat. Anchoring the city's waterfront at its east end, the massive stone August Fitger Brewery, abandoned since it closed in 1972, has been reincarnated as Fitger's

Above: *Canoeing on the Kiwishiwi River in early fall.*
DANIEL J. COX
Left: *An empty cafe in the Iron-Range town of Virginia.*
R. HAMILTON SMITH

Above: *Duluth's Union Depot cum arts center flanked by the oreboat-inspired public library.*
PATRICIA CONDON JOHNSTON
Right: *Sled-dog racing at Ely.*
R. HAMILTON SMITH
Far right: *Sunrise on Lake Kabetogama in Voyageurs National Park.*
TOM TILL

On The Lake, a $12.5 million multi-use development that includes a hotel, restaurants, retail shops and a 160-seat theater.

Once again, Duluth has come up a winner, the transformation being little short of miraculous. For its efforts, Duluth was chosen one of 16 finalists in the 1986-87 All-America Cities competition.

94

The fate of Minnesota's timber wolves currently is in limbo. Except for Alaska and Canada, Minnesota has the only significant population of timber wolves in North America, but the question is how best to protect them. Since passage of the Endangered Species Act in 1966, their numbers have increased, and they have expanded their range into parts of the state where they had not been seen since pioneer days. Approximately 1,200 wolves roam the forests of northeastern Minnesota, preying primarily on white-tailed deer, but they are also a threat to livestock in some areas.

Wildlife biologist L. David Mech, who has made a lifelong career of monitoring Minnesota's wolves, believes the best way to safeguard this threatened species is to allow sportsmen to trap limited numbers of them. Wolves now occupy all of the state's suitable habitat with the result that they are encroaching on populated areas. Besides enraging farmers, this only encourages poaching. As many as 250 wolves are thought to be killed illegally each year for their pelts. A limited harvest would be in the wolves' best interest, Mech maintains.

Numerous conservation groups disagree with Mech, however, arguing that trapping would violate the Endangered Species Act, and a recent federal court decision supports their position. In accord with current regulations, federal agents can and do trap nuisance wolves, while pups must be released. Meantime, state officials would like to see Minnesota's wolf population controlled before livestock predation occurs. It is the best way to prevent illegal killing, they say, and they will continue their efforts to change existing legislation.

One thing will not change. The wolf needs sufficient wild habitat such as that offered by the Boundary Waters Canoe Area and Superior National Forest to insure its survival. Where wolves once roamed the lower 48 states, they now occupy a mere 1 percent of their former range. In Minne-

JEFF VANUGA

sota, they have come to symbolize the wilderness itself. To quote Minnesota writer Sigurd Olson: "If the great, gray timber wolves ever leave the Quetico-Superior, the land will lose its character. It may still be wilderness, but one with savor and uniqueness gone."

CHAPTER 9

NORTHWESTERN MINNESOTA
AN ICE-AGE INHERITANCE

The wide, flat and wonderfully fertile Red River Valley is a legacy of Glacial Lake Agassiz. One of the most productive farming areas in the world, it once was covered by North America's largest ice-margin lake, the southern shore of which can be traced from Browns Valley in a northeastward arc to east of Lake of the Woods.

Glacial Lake Agassiz formed when meltwater from Minnesota's last glacier was impeded to the south by the Big Stone moraine at Browns Valley. At its greatest extent, covering a region of more than 110,000 square miles, Lake Agassiz was more than 700 miles long from its southern shore in western Minnesota to its northern extreme near Hudson Bay. About 12,000 years ago, the lake overflowed the Big Stone moraine, unleashing Glacial River Warren which cut the present Minnesota River Valley. When the glacier later melted farther north, uncovering lower outlets, the River Warren was beheaded, and Lake Agassiz quickly diminished. The extent and subsequent retreating stages of Lake Agassiz are marked by four prominent beaches—low sand, gravel and boulder ridges, generally five to 25 feet high—that run for several hundred miles in northwestern Minnesota.

Unlike other parts of the state, northwestern Minnesota was not shaped by streams eroding and draining its surface. The gently sloping former bed of Glacial Lake Agassiz only encourages its streams and rivers to wander aimlessly. Despite its vast watershed, the Red River of the North is a relatively small stream in a meandering channel that had nothing whatsoever to do with leveling the present Red River Valley.

Lack of topographic diversity typifies the Lake Agassiz plain, but the region has inherited organically rich, moisture-retentive clay soils, evolving from silty lake-deposited sediments and decayed vegetation. Underlying glacial drift is as much as several hundred feet thick, and there is virtually no exposed bedrock. Now planted to a wide diversity of crops, the Red River Valley has been counted one of the world's bread baskets. To the east, where poor drainage hinders agriculture, a vast and beautiful conifer bog blankets much of Lake of the Woods, Roseau, Beltrami and Koochiching counties.

Jutting into Canada about 100 miles east of the North Dakota border, the Northwest Angle is the northernmost piece of land in the contiguous 48 states. After reaching the area by way of Lake Superior, Grand Portage and the border lakes route, Pierre Gaultier de Varennes, Sieur de La Verendrye, built Fort St. Charles, a palisaded enclosure 100'x 60'with four main buildings and a chapel, along the northern edge of the Angle in 1732. La Verendrye, his sons and nephew, were the first Frenchmen in the Red River Valley, where they established at least three fur trading posts. La Verendrye is remembered for his valiant efforts to push French claims to the western sea. Although he never found a Northwest Passage, La Verendrye opened the canoe route between Lake Superior and Lake Winnipeg, exploring westward as far as the Mandan villages along the Missouri River.

Tragedy struck Fort St. Charles in 1736 when a party of 21 Frenchmen, including La Verendrye's son Jean and Jesuit missionary Father Jean Pierre Aulneau, was massacred by hostile Dakota on an island in Lake of the Woods. Their bodies were mutilated, and all of them

were beheaded, the Indians taking the heads of Jean La Verendrye and the priest as trophies. All signs of Fort St. Charles had disappeared by the time a party of Jesuits discovered its original site in the early 1900s, but its location was confirmed by a burial containing 19 skulls and two headless skeletons. Since then, Fort St. Charles has been restored by Minnesota Knights of Columbus, who maintain two housekeeping cabins at the site for visiting clergy.

The first white settlers in the Red River Valley arrived via Hudson Bay. In 1811, with the best intentions,

In the valley of the Red River of the North, whose wandering shape is a legacy of Glacial Lake Agassiz.

Facing page, left: *Train turns to mirage on a hot Northwest Minnesota afternoon.*
Right: *Harvesting wheat in the Red River Valley.* R. HAMILTON SMITH PHOTOS

Red River carts on 3rd St. in St. Paul, at Cheritree and Farwell's hardware store. By this year, 1859, the importance of Red River carts for transport between St. Paul, Pembina and Fort Garry was about to be eclipsed by steamboats on the Red River.
MINNESOTA HISTORICAL SOCIETY

the altruistic Scottish Earl of Selkirk began settling impoverished Scottish crofters on an immense tract of land that took in approximately the present province of Manitoba and the northern parts of North Dakota and Minnesota. Unfortunately, the hundreds of Scottish, Irish, Swiss and German peasants he eventually lured there faced such calamities (including—but not limited to—Indian hostilities, grasshopper plagues, droughts and floods) that many of them left, making their way south to Fort Snelling over the future route of the Red River carts. After living several years in the shadow of the fort, they were forcibly evicted from the military reservation in 1840. Moved downriver a short distance, they became some of St. Paul's first residents.

Once Minnesota Territory was formed, Pembina on the west side of the Red River became an important northern settlement. (While the Red River forms Minnesota's current western boundary north from Lake Traverse, Minnesota Territory took in most of present-day North and South Dakota to the Missouri River.) One of Lord Selkirk's colonies, Pembina was the site of a former British fur post that John Jacob Astor's American Fur Company subsequently acquired. Beginning in 1843 when Henry Sibley started doing business with the enterprising Henry Kittson at Pembina, American trade with the Red River settlements rose sharply.

Albeit a fur trader, Kittson added to his fortunes by transporting merchandise to Canadian customers in the vicinity of Fort Garry at the juncture of the Red and Assiniboine rivers (where Winnipeg is now located), employing Red River carts. Devised by métis people in the Red River Valley, these creaky, two-wheeled wooden carts, pulled by a single ox or pony, came to symbolize Minnesota's northward movement. By the 1850s, annual caravans of as many as 500 or 600 oxcarts were traveling the three Red River trails connecting St. Paul, Pembina and Fort Garry. Arriving in St. Paul laden with buffalo robes and furs for New York and London markets, they returned north piled high with dry goods, clothing, groceries, tobacco and liquor. For all practical purposes, the Red River trails were Minnesota's first roads. Later, railroads and highways used these same routes. Following Indian land cessions, white settlers moved into the Red River Valley in the 1850s. Hoping to win a contract to transport goods north to Canada, St. Paul's fledgling Chamber of Commerce offered a prize of $1,000 to the first person to put a steamboat on the Red River. A clever Yankee named Anson Northrup, a St. Anthony resident, sailed a steamer up the Mississippi to Crow Wing, then dismantled it and hauled it overland with 34 ox teams to the Red River, where he reassembled it and claimed the prize. Soon afterwards, James J. Hill, in partnership with Norman Kittson, who later helped him buy his first railroad, was running steamers on the Red River.

Hill's plan was ingenious. All he needed to do was to build a railroad for transporting freight to the Red River, along which it could continue north by boat. When his St. Paul, Minneapolis & Manitoba line pushed west across Minnesota, then north to the Canadian border in the late 1870s, the empire builder held a winning hand. Two bumper wheat harvests in a row followed, Hill's freight traffic was immense, and immigration to the Northwest swelled. Because of Hill's enthusiastic agents in Scandinavia, a flood of immigrants from Sweden and Norway poured into the Red River Valley.

This was the era of the great "bonanza" wheat farms. Learning of the Red River Valley's amazingly productive cropland, eastern investors bought up huge tracts, often 10,000 acres or more, and brought in hundreds of horses, laborers and new-fangled reapers and threshers to plow, plant and harvest King Wheat. According to Red River Valley folklore, the fields were so long that a worker could start out plowing one furrow in the spring, then harvest his way back in the fall. Produced by the millions of bushels, Red River Valley wheat made Minneapolis a world flour-milling center. But the day of the bonanza farms was short-lived. When wheat prices later dropped, supply being greater than demand, absentee owners divided and sold these immense farms.

Wheat remains an important Red River Valley crop, but farmers also now plant this flat, fertile country to barley, flax, potatoes, sugar beets, sunflowers and vegetables. Minnesota grows more sugar beets than any other

state, with Polk County, its back to North Dakota, the top-producing county. Polk County is also the leading Minnesota grower of sunflowers and barley, the reason Minnesota ranks third nationally in sunflower and barley production. And if you're looking for a bargain in Minnesota farmland, look no farther. The price of farmland in the Red River Valley never rose so drastically in the early 1980s as it did in southern Minnesota; prices peaked at less than $700 an acre, but you can buy an acre today for about $400.

Across the Red River from Fargo, North Dakota, Moorhead is northwestern Minnesota's largest city, having originated as a transportation terminus for, in turn, Red River carts, steamboats and railroads. Dating from 1871, the city is named for Dr. William G. Moorhead of Pennsylvania, a director of the Northern Pacific Railroad. By the early 1880s it was large enough to warrant several hotels, one of these the Grand Pacific, "the pride of

Left: *A wheatfield at harvest time reveals an abstract beauty.*
R. HAMILTON SMITH

Above: *The four-year-old Northern Pacific Colonists Reception House at Glyndon, 1876.*
MINNESOTA HISTORICAL SOCIETY

PRIMEVAL MONARCH
MINNESOTA'S MOOSE

Before white settlement in northern Minnesota, moose were the most common big-game animal in the boreal forests. Although outnumbered by caribou in the extreme northeast, moose were abundant as far west and south as Roseau, Wadena and Chisago counties. Weighing in at up to 1,200 pounds (as much as four or five white-tailed deer), this blackish-brown member of the deer family was an important source of food and clothing for the Indians. Later, during the fur-trade era, moose meat and skins became prized articles of commerce, with large numbers of moose being destroyed by both whites and Indians. In one instance, fur men Radisson and Groseilliers claimed to have killed 600 moose southwest of Lake Superior with the aid of Indians one springtime around 1660.

Moose is an Algonquin word meaning "twig-eater" or "he who eats off." Like the white-tailed deer, the moose is a browser, preferring shrub and second-growth forest. Moose populations declined sharply in Minnesota as a result of logging and fires that produced second-growth forests, encouraging the whitetails to invade former moose range. Ironically, white-tailed deer pose one of the greatest threats to Minnesota's moose population because they harbor brainworm, a parasite that is harmless to them, but fatal to moose. White-tailed deer reached peak numbers in cutover habitats in northern Minnesota in the 1920s and 1930s, and moose numbers diminished markedly at the same time—with most of the decline attributed to infection by brainworm.

Statewide, Minnesota's moose population is estimated at 6,000 to 8,000, the animals thriving in two different habitats: the rocky, lake-dotted boreal forest region of the northeast and the boggy lowland north and west of the Red Lakes. In northwestern Minnesota, a herd of about 400 moose is maintained at Agassiz National Wildlife Refuge near Thief River Falls, a 62,000-acre marsh and woodland wilderness on the glacial lakebed that also harbors 2,000 white-tailed deer, and beavers, muskrats, bobcats, foxes, otters, porcupines, skunks, minks, coyotes, badgers, bears, squirrels, fishers and gray wolves.

Moorhead." Built at a cost of $165,000, it had 140 rooms with connecting baths, and its handsome bar was stocked with "invigorating beverages." (Across the river, North Dakota was dry.) As it happened, the hotel was too "grand" to pay, and it was razed by the mortgage holder, James J. Hill.

Today, with 30,000 residents, Moorhead sees its largest employer in the American Crystal Sugar Company, which refines beet sugar. (Two additional sugar-beet refineries are located in Crookston and East Grand Forks.) Coca Cola has a bottling plant and Anheuser-Busch operates a malting plant. But Moorhead State University, Concordia College and the Moorhead Area Vocational Technical Institute together employ more residents than all the city's agribusinesses combined. Moorhead has a symphony orchestra, opera company, community theater, dance companies and several art galleries. A major new facility is the Heritage-Hjemkomst Interpretive Center, focusing on the history of the Red River Valley, which features the replica Viking ship *Hjemkomst,* the vessel that sailed from Duluth to Norway in 1982.

At 506 Eighth Street South in Moorhead, the Minnesota Historical Society conducts guided tours of the Solomon G. Comstock House, once the showplace of a three-state area. Designed by the Minneapolis firm of Kees and Fisk, it is an early Queen Anne frame house, built in 1883, distinguished by its false half-timbering, pitched roofs and clustered chimneys. Solomon Comstock was a leading Red River Valley entrepreneur and politician, born in Maine in 1842 and trained as a lawyer, who worked closely with James J. Hill, locating townsites for the Great Northern Railroad. His daughter Ada Comstock was the first dean of women at the University of Minnesota and president of Radcliffe College from 1923 to 1943.

In its northeastern reaches, the northwestern section of Minnesota is underlaid with vast deposits of peat which developed on poorly-drained portions of the Glacial Lake Agassiz plain. Minnesota, in fact, has more peat than any other state. There are some 19 million acres of peatlands in the conterminous United States, more than 7 million of which are in Minnesota. Taking in much of Lake of the Woods, Roseau, Beltrami and Koochiching counties, Minnesota's Red Lake Peatland alone covers an area approximately 450 miles square. An important potential source of energy, peat is composed of partially-decayed plant material that has accumulated in a water-saturated environment over a long period of time. Most Minnesota peat began developing on extinct glacial lake beds about 5,000 years ago with the onset of a cooler, moister climate that retarded plant decomposition. The idea of using peat for energy has been around for more than a century in Minnesota. In 1870 a legislative committee recommended using it to fuel locomotives, and the old Phoenix Building in Minneapolis was heated with powdered peat. According to estimates by the Minnesota Geological Survey, Minnesota has 3.6 billion tons of peat suitable for fuel. That is enough peat to supply all of the state's energy needs for 50 years at the present rate of consumption. Dried peat has a heating value similar to lignite, a low-grade coal, and it has much the same sulphur content as western coal.

Few people are in much of a hurry to significantly disturb Minnesota's peatlands, however. To many, these lands represent the state's last true wilderness. A rich vegetative mosaic, including rare orchids and many unusual carnivorous and parasitic plants, peatlands provide the only habitat in the state for several plants and animals. More than 50 wildlife species, including the timber wolf, which have been identified as endangered, threatened or rare on a state-wide level, occur in the peatlands. These same peat bogs also provide habitat for moose, deer, songbirds and several species of grouse, owls and hawks. With peatland ecology so little understood at present, preserving certain peatlands in their natural state will provide a laboratory for ecological research, helpful to mitigating the environmental impact of future development.

There is likewise the archaeological potential of Minnesota's peatlands to consider. Since peatland environment inhibits decomposition, pollen and plant remains laid down during thousands of years provide clues to past climatic and vegetative history. In Europe, nearly perfectly preserved human skeleton remains have been unearthed in peat deposits. In Minnesota, where the state's earliest residents lived on the shores of glacial lakes and rivers before peat deposits began forming, a prehistoric buffalo kill site has been excavated in peatland at Itasca State Park.

While many questions regarding the development and use of peat remain unanswered, the Minnesota Department of Natural Resources urges that state peatlands be managed cautiously for multiple uses including horti-

culture, agriculture, forestry, energy, recreation, scientific study and wildlife habitat. Meanwhile, at least one Minnesota company is exploring the feasibility of developing a large peat gasification plant to produce synthetic natural gas in northern Minnesota. Peat-derived fuel is still relatively expensive to produce, but the cost of manufacturing gas from peat is expected to become more competitive as the cost of natural gas continues to rise. Given growing energy demands and dwindling fossil fuel supplies, it seems likely that Minnesota may soon turn to peat for some of its energy needs.

A cattail bog turning golden in October. JEFF GNASS

Overleaf: *Sunset with Canada geese.*
DANIEL J. COX

General

Blegen, Theodore C. *Minnesota: A History of the State*. Minneapolis: Univ.of Minnesota Pr., 1963.

Borchert, John R. *America's Northern Heartland*. Minneapolis: Univ. of Minnestoa Pr., 1987.

Federal Writers' Project of the Works Progress Administration, comp. *Minnesota: A State Guide*. New York: Viking Press, 1938.

Folwell, William Watts. *A History of Minnesota*. Four volumes. First published in 1920s. Corrected reprints, 1956, 1961, 1969. St. Paul: Minnesota Hist.Soc. Press.

Gebhard, David, and Tom Martinson. *A Guide to the Architecture of Minnesota*. Minneapolis: Univ. of Minnesota Pr., 1977.

Grossman, Mary Ann, ed,. *The Minnesota Almanac;*. 2nd ed.. Taylor Falls, Minn.: John L. Brekke and Sons, 1981.

Holmquist, June Drenning, and Jean A. Brookins. *Minnesota's Major Historic Sites: A Guide*. St. Paul: Minnesota Hist. Soc., 1972.

Larson, Don W. *Land of the Giants: A History of Minnesota Business*. Minneapolis: Dorn Books, 1979.

Lass, William E. *Minnesota: A Bicentennial History*. New York: W. W. Norton, 1977.

The Land

Jones, Evan. *The Minnesota: Forgotten River*. New York: Holt, Rinehart and Winston, 1962.

Ojakangas, Richard W., and Charles L. Matsch, *Minnesota's Geology*. Minneapolis: Univ. of Minnesota Pr., 1982.

Sansome, Constance Jefferson. *Minnesota Underfoot: A Guide to the State's Outstanding Geologic Features*. Edina, Minnesota: Voyageur Press, 1983.*

Waters, Thomas F. *The Streams and Rivers of Minnesota*. Minneapolis: Univ. of Minnesota Pr., 1977.

The People: Indians to Immigrants

Densmore, Frances. *Chippewa Customs*. First published in 1929. Reprint edition. St. Paul: Minnesota Hist. Soc. Pr., 1979.

Ebbott, Elizabeth. *Indians in Minnesota;* 4th ed.. Minneapolis: Univ. of Minnesota Pr., 1985.

Holmquist, June Drenning, ed.. *They Chose Minnesota: A Survey of the State's Ethnic Groups*. St. Paul: Minnesota Hist. Soc. Pr., 1981.

Johnson, Elden. *The Prehistoric Peoples of Minnesota*. St. Paul: Minnesota Hist. Soc., 1969.

Johnston, Patricia Condon. *Minnesota's Irish*. Afton, Minnesota: Johnston Publishing, Inc., 1984.

Johnston, Patricia Condon. *Stillwater: Minnesota's Birthplace*. Afton, Minnesota: Johnston Publishing, Inc., 1982.

Martin, Albro. *James J. Hill and the Opening of the Northwest*. New York: Oxford Univ. Pr., 1976.

Pond, Samuel W. *The Dakota or Sioux in Minnesota as They Were in 1834*. Reprint edition. St. Paul: Minnesota Hist. Soc. Pr., 1986.

Twin Cities

Borchert, John R., et al. *Legacy of Minneapolis: Preservation Amid Change*. Bloomington, Minnesota: Voyageur Press, 1983.*

Flanagan, Barbara. *Minneapolis: City of Lakes and Skyways*. Minneapolis: The Nodin Press, 1975.

Kane, Lucile M., and Alan Ominsky. *Twin Cities: A Pictorial History of Saint Paul and Minneapolis*. St. Paul: Minnesota Hist. Soc. Pr., 1983.

Kunz, Virginia Brainard. *St. Paul: Saga of an American City*. Woodland Hills, California: Windsor Publications, Inc., 1977.

Williams, J. Fletcher. *The History of the City of Saint Paul to 1875*. Reprint edition. St. Paul: Minnesota Hist. Soc. Pr., 1983.

Southeastern Triangle

Clapesattle, Helen. *The Doctors Mayo*. Minneapolis: Univ. of Minnesota Pr., 1941.

Johnston, Patricia Condon. *Pretty Red Wing: Historic River Town*. Afton, Minnesota: Johnston Publishing, Inc., 1983.

Huntington, George. *Robber and Hero: The Story of the Northfield Bank Raid*. Reprint edition. St. Paul: Minnesota Hist. Soc. Pr., 1986.

Mather, Cotton, and Ruth Hale. *Prairie Border Country*. Prescott, Wisconsin: Trimbelle Press, 1980.

Southwestern Minnesota

Anderson, Gary Clayton, and Alan R. Woolworth, eds. *Through Dakota Eyes: Narrative Accounts of the Minnesota Indian War of 1862*. St. Paul: Minnesota Hist. Soc. Pr., 1987.

Carley, Kenneth. *The Sioux Uprising of 1862*. St. Paul: The Minnesota Hist. Soc., 1976.

Meyer, Roy W. *History of the Santee Sioux: United States Indian Policy on Trial*. Lincoln: Univ. of Nebraska Press, 1967.

Minnesota's Heartland

Blegen, Theodore C. *The Kensington Rune Stone: New Light on an Old Riddle*. St. Paul: Minnesota Hist. Soc., 1968.

Keillor, Garrison. *Lake Wobegon Days*. New York: Viking, 1985.

Lindbergh, Charles A. *Boyhood on the Upper Mississippi: A Reminiscent Letter*. St. Paul, Minnesota Hist. Soc., 1972.

The Arrowhead Region

Gilman, Carolyn. *Where Two Worlds Meet: The Great Lakes Fur Trade*. St. Paul: Minnesota Hist. Soc. Pr., 1982.

Jaques, Florence Page. *Francis Lee Jaques: Artist of the Wilderness World*. New York: Doubleday, 1973.

Kimball, Joe. *Secrets of the Congdon Mansion*. Minneapolis: Jaykay Publishing Inc., 1985.

Koblas, John J. *Sinclair Lewis: Home at Last*. Bloomington, Minnesota: Voyageur Press, 1981.*

Northwestern Minnesota

Drache, Hiram M. *The Day of the Bonanza: A History of Bonanza Farming in the Red River Valley of the North*. Fargo: North Dakota Institute for Regional Studies, 1964.

Gilman, Rhoda R., et al. *The Red River Trails: Oxcart Routes Between St. Paul and the Selkirk Settlement, 1820-1870*. St. Paul: Minnesota Hist. Soc. Pr., 1979.

Weygant, Sister Noemi. *Fort St. Charles: The History, Discovery and Restoration of Minnesota's Forgotten Fort*. Bloomington, Minnesota: Voyageur Press, 1981.*

For More Information

Regional brochures, brochures on individual communities and resort areas, and maps are available from the Minnesota Office of Tourism, 375 Jackson St., Room 250, St. Paul, MN 55101.

For specific information on where to go and what to see, call the Minnesota Travel Information Center at these toll-free numbers. Outside Minnesota: (800) 328-1461; in Minnesota: (800) 652-9747; Minneapolis/St. Paul: 296-5029.

*Voyageur Press now is located in Stillwater, Minnesota.

AMERICAN GEOGRAPHIC PUBLISHING

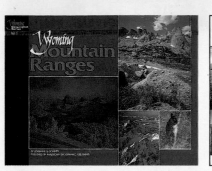

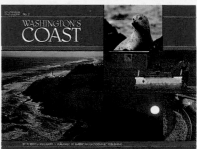

EACH BOOK HAS ABOUT 100 PAGES, 11" X 8¹/₂" 120 TO 170 COLOR PHOTO-GRAPHS

Enjoy, See, Understand America State by State

American Geographic Publishing
Geographic Series of the States

Lively, colorful, beautifully illustrated books specially written for these series explain land form, animals and plants, economy, lifestyle and history of each state or feature. Generous color photography brings each state to life and makes each book a treat to turn to frequently. The geographic series format is designed to give you more information than coffee-table photo books, yet so much more color photography than simple guide books.

Each book includes:
- Colorful maps
- Valuable descriptions and charts of features such as volcanoes and glaciers
- Up-to-date understanding of environmental problems where man and nature are in conflict
- References for additional reading, agencies and offices to contact for more information
- Special sections portraying people in their homes, at work, in the countryside

for more information write:
American Geographic Publishing
P.O. Box 5630
Helena, Montana 59604